D1126359

the riddle song and other rememberings

REBECCA McCLANAHAN

the riddle song & other rememberings

THE UNIVERSITY OF GEORGIA PRESS

ATHENS AND LONDON

Published by the University of Georgia Press

Athens, Georgia 30602

© 2002 by Rebecca McClanahan

All rights reserved

Photograph by Mary Ruth Moore

Set in Bembo

Printed and bound by Thomson-Shore

The paper in this book meets the guidelines for permanence
and durability of the Committee on Production Guidelines
for Book Longevity of the Council on Library Resources.

Printed in the United States of America

06 05 04 03 02 C 5 4 3 2 1

Library of Congress Cataloging-in-Publication Data

McClanahan, Rebecca.

The riddle song and other rememberings / Rebecca McClanahan.

p. cm.

ISBN 0-8203-2353-5 (alk. paper)

1. McClanahan, Rebecca—Family. 2. Poets, American—
20th century—Family relationships. 3. Poets, American—
20th century—Biography. I. Title.

PS3554.E9274 Z468 2002

811'.54—dc21

[B]

2001043071

British Library Cataloging-in-Publication Data available

in memory of Bessie Mounts Cosby, 1880–1979

contents

preface ix

aunt 1

the uncles 10

the riddle song: a twelve part lullaby 18

the cloud's immaculate folds 56

dependent 64

earth, air, fire, and father 80

hatching 92

life and death, yes and no,
and other mysteries in mansfield, ohio 99

the weather 117

with my father in space-time 127

two autumns, one story 141

the other mother 149

good-bye to all this 166

acknowledgments 191

preface

THE FOLLOWING ESSAYS evolved over the space of many years. Each was shaped as a complete, independent work, but over time it became clear that, taken together, the essays formed a whole larger than the sum of individual parts. Since each essay was originally written to stand alone, some readers may choose to sample the selections in no particular order. However, the essays are not randomly ordered but rather arranged so that they build upon each other. Like the recurring lines of "The Riddle Song," the folk tune my mother used to sing to us from the driver's seat of one station wagon or another, the essays loop back upon themselves. Images resurface, places are revisited, the same people keep showing up at the door of every tale. And the same questions keep asking themselves.

This book is not, strictly speaking, a memoir. It does not proceed chronologically and its primary focus is not the *events* of a life but rather the questions arising from those events. At times the questions are personal and domestic, circumscribed by the rituals of family, home, and marriage: What manner of man is my father, my uncle, my husband? What womanly secrets were passed between my grandmother and mother, my aunts, my sisters? How did the past and present places of my life—the family farm, military bases, cemeteries, universities, hospital rooms—help shape the person I've become?

At other times, the questions move from personal to public, from specific to general, from *I* to *you* to *us:* How do we navigate the spaces between ourselves and others? How do our lives snap into place inside the larger puzzle? How does time have its way with us? Each of us is an *enigma;* the word is rooted in the Greek *ainigma,* born of *tale* or *story.* One way to deepen our personal and public riddles is through the stories we tell. Here are mine.

the riddle song and other rememberings

aunt

YESTERDAY we spent the afternoon at the lawyer's office, drawing up our wills. My husband's took only a few minutes. "I'm
taking all my parts with me," Donald said when he got to the organ donor section. "Everything else goes to you, if I die first." *If
you survive him,* is the way the lawyer put it. I laughed, thinking of
Great-aunt Bessie. Every morning she'd study the obituaries.
"Listen to this," she'd say, smoothing the crease in the newspaper.
"Mr. Etheridge is survived by his wife Matilda. Doesn't that just
slay you? *Survived by.* Any wife who can survive Bo Etheridge,
she deserves to get everything."

After an hour Donald shook his head, lifted his hands in surrender. I had been pausing at each line, considering the left eye-
ball, the right. I want every organ, every possession accounted
for. For one niece, the piano and gold pocket watch. For another,
Aunt Bessie's century-old baby shoes, black leather with button
clasps. Who will want my diaries, notebooks, the family reunion
of words collected in my books? My property will be put into a
trust to be divided equally for the education of the nephews and
nieces. There are fifteen of them, a tribe of borrowed children,
mine for the asking. So I ask. One by one I try them on, wear

them a day, a week. The best of both worlds, everyone says. Enjoy them, but when you've had enough, send them home where they belong. I think of the fledgling: It is wrong to touch a baby bird, to leave your scent, for when the mother returns to the nest, she will know you have been there.

MAYBE SOME OF US were meant from the beginning to be aunts. Maybe we are too weak to bear the full weight of a child. How many times have I had this nightmare—a baby being sucked from my hands out an open window, and me left holding the sack of its nightgown. Maybe the powers-that-be give children to those who can survive the love, who know when to let go, who won't die if they suddenly find themselves holding an empty nightgown. My mother must have known from the start that I would never have children. I needed a guide for that other road, the road my mother had not taken.

The night Aunt Bessie arrived, I was sitting cross-legged on my bed, reviewing the events leading up to World War II for the test the next day. When I heard gravel in the driveway, I walked to the window and lifted a slat on the venetian blind. Dad was opening the door to the passenger side, and I watched as she emerged from semidarkness into the glare of the porch light. In a few minutes she stood in the doorway of my room holding a brown suitcase, her navy blue wool coat stuffed so tight that the buttonholes squinted. And as I watched, an amazing thing happened. She started out plump, then sweater by sweater, blouse by blouse, skirt by skirt, she shrank until she stood before me—a hunched, scrawny sparrow of a woman in a brown taffeta dress with glittery buttons.

I ran into the kitchen where my mother was stirring a pot of stew. "Why me?" I screamed. Mother just shrugged and smiled, as if that were answer enough.

"Why me? Why not Claudia or Jennifer?"

"They're night owls, honey. Aunt Bessie's an early riser like you."

BY THE THIRD DAY the battle lines were drawn. I divided the dresser. Lining the mirror on my side was a row of eight dolls that I dutifully dressed each morning, a three-tiered jewelry box that played "Around the World in Eighty Days," a cache of plastic pop beads and initial bracelets, a pair of clip-on earrings I was not yet allowed to wear, and a grainy five-by-seven of Ricky Nelson that I had scissored from *Teen Magazine*. On her side, arranged on a doily, was everything she had unzipped from the satin pouch of her suitcase: a gold pocket watch, tweezers, a box of Polident, a framed picture of Lord Byron, a huge black purse with a clamp like an alligator's jaw, and a photograph of a sad young woman. My mother said it was Aunt Bessie's wedding picture, but I didn't believe her. I had seen plenty of wedding pictures—the bride radiant in a flouncy veil and pearls, her white-toothed groom bending over her as they cut the cake together, hand over hand, grinning into the camera.

No, I decided, the woman in this picture could not possibly be a bride. She was standing alone in a shapeless gown. Her head was bare, her hair yanked into a knot. Not the silky chignon the women on *Wagon Train* wore, just a tight thin knot without ribbon or other adornment. She was turned sideways, her head bent low. And instead of holding a bridal bouquet with streamers, she held a single rose, which drooped as if it were falling from her hand. My mother assured me there *had* been a husband and that he loved Aunt Bessie so much he built her a home in Stockwell, Indiana, with an oval window embedded in the front door, a home filled with beautiful things like linen napkins pressed just so in the drawer of a heavy chest that stood in the entry hall. I didn't believe that either. "If Aunt Bessie was really married," I said, "where are the grandchildren?"

"She had one baby," my mother answered. "But it died before it was born. It was a long, long time ago." I could not imagine history that ancient.

BY THE THIRD WEEK I was wishing Aunt Bessie dead, or at least transported to my sisters' room. I hated her oldness—the swish of taffeta down the hall, the clonk of heavy heels, and the mechanical clack of her loose dentures. Many dentists had tried to adjust the dentures, but Aunt Bessie had a crooked jaw, and when my father finally located a specialist and paid hundreds of dollars for two sets that actually fit, she lost them both—one in a field in Pennsylvania where we'd stopped to pick blackberries and one at sixty miles per hour, in the cubicle bathroom of a Greyhound bus. Finally in desperation my father settled for an economy set. Every night I'd pull the covers over my head and try to sleep as she propped up a pillow, switched on the night-light attached to the headboard, and clacked her way through *National Geographic,* Browning's "Last Duchess," seed catalogs, fairy tales, detective magazines, *Reader's Digest,* whatever she could find. She always ended with Byron. She didn't read silently with her eyes like normal people, but she didn't exactly read aloud either. She simply moved her crooked jaw a little and whispered, just enough movement to set her dentures clacking. That was the last sound I heard at night.

And in the morning I'd wake to the fizz of Polident in a glass by the bed. I'd look up through bleary eyes for my first sight of the day—Aunt Bessie leaning at the waist and pouring her powdered breasts into a stiff brassiere. She'd stand by the mirror and pluck a stray whisker from her chin. This disturbed me: a woman with whiskers. And not only whiskers. All over her body, hair sprouted in unlikely places—from her nostrils, her ears, migrating from the places where I judged it should be, the places where it was just beginning on me. She never shaved her legs, yet they were smooth as the legs of a rubber doll. The pits of her underarms were hairless. Even her eyebrows were missing. She'd sketch them in each morning with a small black pencil that she kept rolled in a hankie. *Old maid,* I'd hiss beneath the covers. Then when she was gone, swishing down the hall, I'd crawl from bed and dress for school, where girls with real eyebrows were gathering in the halls.

I HAD LONG SINCE given up my dolls, but every Sunday I volunteered to dress Aunt Bessie for church. She was the only grown-up small enough and old enough to be under my control. Looking back, I wonder why she let me use her. Maybe she liked the attention. Maybe the feel of young hands was so comforting that she bore the humiliation.

I started with her hair. It wasn't the silver floss of my grandmother nor the spongy blue-gray of widows whose hair is constructed each Saturday morning. Bessie's hair was the muddied gray of leftover snow. She'd lean over the kitchen sink and I'd lather up the Prell. Wet, her hair was fine as a baby's. Her scalp beneath my fingers was pink and exposed, and I could hardly stand to look at it. I'd squeeze the wet hair into a towel, then co-

erce a rattail comb through, making parts for the yellow rollers—
a row down the center from her forehead to the nape of her
neck. Then pin curls on each side, above her ears.

It was the year of bonnet hair dryers; my mother had gotten
one for Christmas. When I placed the plastic daisy bonnet onto
Aunt Bessie's head, it slipped toward her eyes, over the scratch-
ings of what was left of her eyebrows, their shapely arches having
long since swirled down the drain with the Prell. I'd set the timer
for ten minutes. With each minute, her face reddened and
chapped and she talked louder and louder as if it were *my* ears
that were covered. When the timer went off, I unrolled the curlers one by one and for a minute she was a Shirley Temple doll,
the ringlets tight and shiny from the heat. Then the artistry, the
teasing and back-combing at the crown to give her the fullness
I'd seen in *Ladies' Home Journal*. Then two curls on either side of
her forehead. I'd swirl them inward until they resembled ram's
horns. "Cover your eyes!" I'd shout, and Bessie's hands would
jump to her face while I sprayed Aqua Net until she choked and
begged "No more!" I'd pat her hair, shoot one final spray, and she
would smile. A little blush on her cheeks, a little pink lipstick.
She'd replace the eyebrows herself while I held the mirror.

Bessie's hands were strong and fearsome, her yellowed nails
like talons curving in. The manicure was the final challenge: the
taming of a wild thing. First I clipped the thick nails, then filed
them into ovals. I rubbed cream into her hands and fingers. Her
skin was thin, stretched over knuckles knotty as roots, nothing
left but bone and gristle. I'd choose Avon, some childish pink or
coral, and begin painting the nails. Two coats. Blow on them to
dry. Then the dress. The black crepe or the navy blue taffeta?
Maybe the white blouse with a cameo pin. I chose for this Sun-

day a flowery chintz my mother had made, pale green with yellow zinnias and a ruffled lace collar. "Fine," Bessie said, and I slipped the dress over her head, over the safety-pinned strap of her brassiere and past her crooked hip. I zipped up the back and she was done.

I GREW three inches that year, sailing past Aunt Bessie's lopsided shoulders. The waistbands of my dresses rose; saddle shoes that were fine one morning pinched my toes the next. I was Alice in Wonderland, a fever dream pulsing out of control. It didn't surprise my mother. "Kids grow at night," she said matter-of-factly. "That's why they wake up hungry. It's hard work." One night I woke with excruciating pain in my calves, as if my legs were being stretched on a rack. I kicked off the covers and grabbed my knees, pulling my calves in close. The night-light switched on above my head and Aunt Bessie sat up, turning her face toward me. She was a drawing pad sketch, a gesture, a jot, the mere suggestion of a face. Eyebrows, teeth, the hair-sprayed pouf of morning hair were missing.

She sighed a self-satisfied sigh, as if she'd been anticipating this moment all her life. "Growing pains," was all she said, yet even that was garbled, delivered, as it was, toothless. She creaked from her side of the bed and walked in semidarkness to my side. She rubbed her arthritic hands together. Carefully she folded back the covers and touched my shoulder, coaxing me to turn. Then she rummaged in the headboard shelf and I smelled wintergreen as she squeezed Ben-Gay onto her hands.

Why I gave in so easily, I still don't know. In daylight she was the last person I wanted, the last person I would have imagined touching me. I could have called for my mother; she surely would have come. But I was helpless in the pain and confusion of this newest trick my body was playing, and Aunt Bessie's hands went right for the hurting place. They kneaded and rubbed and tamed the pulsing muscles of my calves. Her knotted hands, the protruding veins, the fingernails I'd painted pink just that morning. She squeezed more ointment from the tube, warmed it between her palms, and began again to rub my calves. After a while, the pain stopped. My tears stopped. And, for the moment, I stopped growing.

NIGHTS when Donald is working, I drive across town to see my niece and nephew, delighting in the small hands running a brush through my hair or slapping red polish on my nails. "Walk on my back," I say to my niece, so I can feel her plump feet kneading the kinks. Yesterday she called me into the bathroom to read her a "potty story" while she sat on the toilet. Her pudgy hands gripped the rim of the seat, and her training pants had slid to her feet. The skin of her thighs was translucent. Beneath it ran a fine river of blue vein. Sometimes I crawl into my nephew's bed and curl behind him, press into his warm back and touch his chest, feeling the heartbeat, holding my next breath until I feel his. Last month when he turned two, the outside world found him. It landed in dirt creases on the back of his neck. While I wasn't looking, he learned to sweat, and now instead of the powdery baby scent, his smell is the smell of a wet puppy.

I RECENTLY DISCOVERED in my parents' antique trunk a leather diary marked 1897. It is Aunt Bessie's diary. In it are recorded the small moments of her seventeenth year. The handwriting is as eccentric and unpredictable as she was, at times painstaking in its perfection, at other times scrawling and nearly illegible. There are entries of anger and self-pity, loneliness and disappointment, then sudden wild-geese flights of joy. She wishes for the words to come more easily. She longs for the power to express the sting of a sleigh ride, the red burn of sunset, the taste of oyster soup and apples. Usually she borrows the words of others, Longfellow and Byron mostly, only occasionally breaking into songs of her own, recalling the gleam of sun on a field "ridged with frost" or a sky "cloudless except for a few fleecy ones in the east." As I read the diary, it begins to make sense—my hunger for words, my very choice of vocation. I want to thank her but she is not here.

The night nurse said she would call for us, the grand-nieces and -nephews, her voice down the hospital corridor unrolling our many names, beginning and ending with mine. She died alone, between shifts. A stranger dressed her and parted her hair and brushed rouge across her gray cheeks. She was buried on a muddy March afternoon, just a few miles from her birthplace. Now all these years later I hold her to me—a tribal instinct perhaps. Or perhaps I simply want to give back some of the words to the young woman in the diary. I sit in my study where shelves of books line the green walls. I finger the dictionaries and search for what lies beneath: aunt. From old French, *ante,* an offshoot, hall leading toward the main room. Latin root, *amma:* mother. Or *amare:* to love. As in *amigo,* as in *amour.* As in *amateur,* one who works for the bare love of it.

the uncles

THEY WERE BULKY SHADOWS with hats, their faces lost in the smoke of cigarettes and mumbled conversation. Uncle Ivan had a job raking rivers. I heard him say that all bodies turn bloated, and except for the way they float (women face-up, men face-down) you can't tell a man from a woman. In the hallway outside the den where my uncles gathered at the pool table, I crouched in a corner to listen. My chest was still flat as a boy's, and when my hair was wet and slicked back I looked more like my brothers than my sisters. I knew this would not last. In the kitchen the aunts, adrift in the steam from boiling pots, loaded oval platters. I sat in the hallway halfway between, watching the fog from the separate rooms meet for a moment, then escape through the vent above my head.

Today is the color of that smoky hallway. Three states away, my family is burying another uncle. Ivan is gone, and Leland and Dick and Robert and John. Only in dreams do they return, their spirits like huge overcoats floating above me. My aunts continue in this world, surviving as farm widows do. They have stepped gracefully through the decades and arrived in the nineties, having long ago exchanged their manure boots and Sunday high heels for the cushioned white athletic shoes that carry them to the mall and back. Even the dead aunts survive. Their spirits, unlike the spirits of the uncles, are not bound by the limitations of dream but return in daylight hours, in dresses and recipes and advice handed down. One aunt lives in the pattern of Blue Willow plates, another in the afghan I pull over my feet at night. Always their memory comes housed in body, their spirits fastened to the homely labors of this earth. Forty years since I was a child and still the aunts are here, surrogate mothers stirring my soup and telling me stories and patting me into bed.

"Every man is a piece of the continent," John Donne wrote. "Any man's death diminishes me." Yet however connected I am to my aunts and however much I mourn their passing, I do not feel diminished by their deaths; I feel enlarged, as if I'm finally growing into the space reserved for me. We fit into each other like Russian *matryoshka* dolls, each new generation of women locked within the old. When an aunt dies, the larger doll that houses me is lifted off, and I become the larger doll inside which my niece is nesting. When I die, my niece will throw off the shell that was my life and, in so doing, will not diminish, but enlarge. I don't know if my brothers feel this sense of enlargement, this growing into their assigned spaces, on the occasions of our uncles' deaths. As for me, each time another uncle dies, I feel whole pieces of myself breaking off and floating from me, and I mourn not merely the man himself but all that is lost with him.

I THINK of the lost uncles the way I think of the lakes of my childhood, uncharted territories whose mysteries can never be exhausted. Creeks were common on my grandparents' farm and I quickly tired of them; there were no surprises to be discovered.

The creek, warmed by the sun, was a happy place to play, but the water was so shallow and clear that not even a stick stirred into the bed could muddy the creek into mystery: I could see right through to the bottom, count each pebble and root and fish. It was the lake that filled my imagination and an acre or so of Uncle John's land. We'd catch bream that danced on the end of the line, and once my foot found a smooth flat stone that miraculously transformed into a turtle. I was both delighted and terrified by the lake, but my terror, like the lake's hidden currents, only served to pull me farther in. I took the first steps gingerly, my feet sinking into soft mud, my teeth rattling as the water rose toward my shoulders, then above. Now there was nothing to do but paddle, treading the black water that unexpectedly turned icy, then just as quickly warm and comforting as bath water. Unable to touch bottom, I dog-paddled until my legs began to twitch from fatigue. Then suddenly an unseen island collided with my knees and I stood upright, laughing, Queen of the Mountain, surrounded by how many more undersea surprises?

Perhaps because my uncles remained distant and mysterious in life, I feel compelled to search for them now that they are dead. As a child I had few opportunities to be alone with my uncles. They always seemed to be leaving—waving from John Deere tractors, from eighteen-wheelers and pickup trucks, from dark sedans with heavy doors that slammed shut as they pulled away. When they were home, they were in the fields, or laying fence, or surrounded by their wives and children who claimed first attention rights. I never exchanged intimate conversation with the uncles as I did with the aunts, with whom I often shared beds or an adjoining slot on the two-seater outhouse. The thoughts and private concerns of my uncles remained as alien to me as their tall straight bodies encased in overalls and rubber hip boots.

As I grew into adolescence, the bodies of my aunts became as familiar as my own, and as they softened and broadened with age, they came to belong to me in a way the bodies of my uncles never will. One day not too long from now, I may be called upon to nurse an aunt toward health or death, as my mother nursed Aunt Bessie. My uncles died apart from me, alone in faraway hospitals or in the care of their wives and daughters, and I am left to reconstruct the missing pieces of their lives through stories told by their surviving women. Of course it's impossible to reconstruct the actual men; I'd be tempted to exaggerate their strengths, minimize their weaknesses. This is a natural inclination, and forgivable—to consider a loved one larger in death than he was in life. Pathologists report that a corpse laid out always measures a little more than the height of the person when alive. Perhaps even the miserable suicides Uncle Ivan dragged from rivers finally reached their full stature in death, for mourners often surfaced with the bodies' discoveries, belatedly paying a debt of love and attention.

I doubt that my uncles knew how much I loved them. How could they have known, when I've yet to measure the depth of the loss? It grows with each recovered letter scribbled by an uncle's hand, each half-remembered incident unlocked in photographs or dreams, each story I beg from my aunts or mother. My favorite passageway to their lives is through the tales of their childhoods. In this way, I break the hard casing of man and free the boy inside. Merrill, my mother's oldest brother, raised rabbits when he was small. His prizes were a male and female—of a rare breed called Flemish giant—that he bought with his hard-earned chore money. He named the female Molly; the name of the male has long been forgotten. Every time Molly had babies, as my mother remembers, she had "an army of them," and after a while Merrill got tired of feeding them, cleaning their cages, chasing them when they got out. Suddenly there were too many Flemish giants running around, their growing numbers suggesting that maybe they weren't that special after all. Besides, a nine-year-old boy had better things to do than mother an army of rabbits. So one day Merrill let them loose. Molly, who had grown domesticated over her year's association with Merrill, continued to stay near the house, but her husband and children scattered into the woods, eventually mating with more common breeds of wild rabbits. Word quickly spread to local hunters that there were giant rabbits to be had in the Sanderses' woods, and for months the air was alive with the crack of rifles. Yet even though times were lean and my mother's family often had to do without meat, Merrill convinced his father and brother not to hunt Molly's progeny. "It just didn't seem right to him," my mother recalls. When old Molly was killed by the family dog, my grandmother took her death as an exception, cooking and dressing Molly and placing her proudly on the best platter. My mother was a small child at the time, but she still remembers the silence at that dinner table. All eyes were on the rabbit, browned and glistening and set ceremoniously in the center of the table, but no one except my grandmother—who ate more from stubborn pride than hunger—would take a bite.

I love the boy who refused to eat his pet rabbit. From the seed of this small act would grow the man who would become my uncle, a man who, like the other men in my family, respected unspoken boundaries. None of my uncles ever hurt me; in this, I am more fortunate than many women. One of my friends had an uncle who did terrible things to her, and only now is she learning how to hate his memory, hate *him* for taking advantage of her love and trust. This has been a difficult step, since, as she once told me, to indict her uncle is to indict a portion of herself. Even Hamlet, though he cursed his "Uncle Father" and plotted his death, was unable to kill Claudius when the opportunity finally presented itself. Perhaps in Claudius he saw a reflection of his dead father—for is not our paternal uncle our father, once removed? Or twice, if the uncle is our grandfather's brother. And our maternal uncle is our mother, once removed. We sense, watching him, that he is the closest our mother ever came to being a man. Studying my uncle's profile—the bump in his nose or the slice of chin—I imagine the form my mother might have taken had the coin of genetics been tossed differently. I've often wondered how much of my mother was carried in my uncles— what portion of her gentleness, her strengths and fears.

My mother's likeness was most clearly seen in Uncle Leland, the younger of her brothers. He had my mother's smile and easy appreciation of the present moment, but just when you thought you had his full attention, his left eye would leave on its own journey, as if he'd glimpsed some peripheral brightness just out of range. Leland was a farmer because his father had been a farmer, and his older brother, and that was all he knew to be. He had no talent for animal husbandry; he treated the livestock like pets. What gave him joy were the housekeeping duties surrounding his modest farm—repairing gates and painting sheds and polishing his tractor. His attention was a domestic, housewifely attention to detail, and his grounds and outbuildings were meticulous.

The actual farming—the plotting and harrowing and planting and harvesting—was secondary, a means to an end. One year when the soybean crop surprised him, he bought a Hammond organ and taught himself to play. Had he not been a man burdened with the world's expectations, he might have been content to sit inside his neat and polished house, playing turn-of-the-century love songs, his wild eye grazing a place far off.

For many months before the kidney disease was diagnosed, Leland didn't know he was ill; he felt only a weakening, a slow siphoning of strength. Then one day, while walking across the field to open the gate for the cows, his knees buckled and he went down. Hours later he woke in what must have seemed a heaven of cows. The Guernseys had gathered around him, in curiosity or puzzlement, their limpid brown eyes staring down at him. His first impulse was fear—as a boy he'd been kicked clean through the barn wall by the hind legs of his father's horse, and for months he wore her hoofprints on his belly—but soon he saw the cows meant no harm. His brother Merrill had arrived by then; he helped Leland to his feet and back to the house. Within weeks, Leland lost the use of his kidneys and was hooked to a dialysis machine that rolled on wheels wherever he went, which wasn't far. At times the pain was acute, and though Leland never recovered his strength, his humor remained intact. "My dog," he called the bag that held the wastes coursing from his bloodstream—and he'd give the bag a gentle kick.

LELAND died at an inconvenient time, or so I remember. I thought I couldn't afford to take off work, or buy the ticket for a plane that would have flown me to the memorial service three states away. I sent flowers, calling out my credit card number to a stranger who wired the message to my uncle's hometown florist who delivered the arrangement to my aunt, who later wrote me a thank-you card provided by the funeral home. I regret missing Leland's funeral, as I regret missing the funerals of the other uncles. They stand apart in death as they did in life. Not long ago, during a difficult and lonely time in my life, one of my friends, a married man, sent a letter of support and affection. "I send my avuncular love," he wrote, "which is unfortunately all I can give." There was a tone of dismissal in the statement, as if the love of an uncle was somehow less than what I needed or wanted. My friend couldn't have known that avuncular love was exactly what I craved, that its loss was what I continue to mourn. In the dream in which my uncles return, their spirits hover, dark overcoats that open protectively above me. One by one the uncles place on my head their heavy hats, which slide down over my eyes. I slip into one overcoat, then another. The empty sleeves shroud my arms and for a moment I am inside their lives. I feel the coolness of the satin lining, smell in the hat bands the reservoir of tobacco and motor oil and freshly cut meadow grasses. I reach out, wanting to be picked up, to be swung in a circle high above their heads, rocked in the laughter that rolls from their throats.

the riddle song: a twelve part lullaby

I gave my love a cherry that had no stone

HOLLY ENTERS THE ROOM, panting. "Sorry I'm late," she says between gasps. "I wanted a good uterus to show you." Holly is always misplacing her visual aids. She plops down into the only remaining seat in the room, a bright orange beanbag. "Have you all been practicing? Remember, breathing is everything." Gasp. "July will be here before you know it." Beside me, my sister giggles. Holly, our instructor, does not inspire confidence. She has miscarried three times and has recently undergone a hysterectomy, but her perpetually round stomach makes her a natural for Lamaze. I'm the only woman in the room with a flat stomach, and Holly holds this against me. The first week of class, we all made name tags—blue for fathers, pink for mothers, a baby rattle floating by our names and due dates. There was no color for aunts, so I made a blue tag. Holly did not approve. Now she surveys the room, taking roll with her eyes. She stops at my sister. "So, Lana, you're really serious about having *two* coaches?"

Lana laughs and pats her belly. "I need all the help I can get." A year ago, her daughter Hanah was born Caesarean. As they wheeled Lana out of the operating room, she raised her head from the gurney. "Next time, I'm going to do it the right way," she said, lifting her hand in a pale fist of victory. In the recovery room, she kept on. "I should have prepared more. If I'd exercised, if I hadn't been so lazy. I should have gone to Lamaze." Nothing Jim or I said would soothe her. She was certain she had failed, that a C-section was some kind of cheating. So, six months ago when she discovered she was pregnant again, Lana began plotting her course. I tried to talk her out of it, showing her the articles I'd xeroxed from the medical journals at the library. I'd read that a vaginal birth could be dangerous after a Caesarean, and our family history of childbirth had made me wary. But the more I tried to convince Lana, the more determined she became. "What are you, some kind of expert?" she said. "Lighten up. Do you want to help coach or not?"

Holly wriggles out of the beanbag chair. It makes a scrunching sound as she stands to join the mothers-to-be in their discussion circle. Jim takes my arm and escorts me to the next room where the dads are gathering. In our group is a plumber, an auto parts worker, a banker, another carpenter besides Jim, and a salesman named Earl who always has a joke ready. "Yes, I've decided to keep working," Earl is saying. "Right up till the end."

"Me too," I say. The other dads laugh, lean back on the extra pillows we've brought for the exercise session. We're supposed to be talking about our wives, their mood swings, the breathing sessions we were assigned to practice last week.

The banker begins. "Victoria thinks Lamaze is a bad idea. There's nothing natural about childbirth, she says. She wants to sleep through it. I tell her one day she'll be glad we did it this way, but she hates pain, what can I say? Just the thought of it brings on an asthma attack."

"We had a fight this week about the nursery," says Steve the plumber. "Stacy wants crayon colors. What the hell are crayon colors? I'd already bought the blue paint. She made me take it back."

"Goddamned nurseries." It's Earl again. "We've been sanding the floors all week. The kid's gonna be born in a cloud of dust."

"And not only crayon colors," continues Steve. "You know that restaurant, the one with the model train that runs on the ceiling? Stacy wants one like it for the nursery. So the baby will have something to watch. What if the engine derails? It could fall on the baby. She's just not thinking straight."

The auto parts salesman, who seems not to notice that his name tag is upside down, takes off his glasses and wipes them on his sleeve. He speaks softly, with hesitation. "It's our third try," he says. "Sometimes I think it's not meant to be." There is a long pause. Earl clears his throat. The salesman looks down at the carpet and shakes his head. "Maybe God's trying to tell us something, you know?" I have a sudden urge to take his hand, to say something, but what right do I have? He puts his glasses back on and turns to Jim. People in trouble are always turning to Jim. He exudes calm, his exterior a smooth glassy sea to my sister's ruffled currents. Nothing disturbs me, I will cope, everything will be all right, his face is saying. But his left sneaker is alive, vibrating with nerves wound too tight. He's been reading the articles, too. A few days before, I'd met him after school for coffee. "Can't you talk her out of it?" I'd said. "Lana doesn't look good. She looks tired."

"She's eight months pregnant and she has a one-year-old. She's supposed to look tired."

"What if something happens? Things happen." For an instant, I saw my mother leaning against the padded headboard, her black hair spidered with gray, the bloodied sheets stuffed behind the door.

"Lana's healthy as a horse. Besides," he continued, a boyish grin forming at the side of his mouth, "if she has a C-section, you'll miss out again. This could be your last chance." He was right. My other sisters were done with babies; my brothers' wives too. And I had yet to be in a delivery room.

"Visual aid time!" Holly sings out, and we move to the next room to join the mothers. At the front of the room, an easel is covered with a white cloth, its skinny tripod legs splayed beneath. When we're all seated, Holly waits a moment for an appropriate silence, then, with a flourish of plump hands ("Ta-dah!"), whips off the cloth, unveiling a chart labeled "Cervical Dilation." Ten openings are cut into the chart, marked from one to ten. Holly moves behind the chart. In a moment one dimpled hand emerges through the ten-centimeter opening. She waves, and a chorus of oohs and ahs ripples through the group. "Miss July!" Earl hoots. "Va-va-voom. I see why they call her a ten." Everyone laughs.

Now from her sack of miracles, Holly unwraps a pink plastic womb, holds it aloft like an urn. She hands it to the auto parts salesman, whose upside-down name tag I can now make out as either Dirk or Dick. He holds the womb for a moment, then passes it to his wife, a sad-looking woman with ragged nails. As the womb makes its way around the circle the laughter slowly diminishes, until, by the time the womb gets to Jim, there is a prayerlike silence. A communion silence, the passing of a holy thing. Jim hands the womb to me, but caught in the center of eyes I fumble, drop it onto the floor. Holly clears her throat and glares. I retrieve the womb and pass it carefully to Lana.

I gave my love a chicken that had no bone

A FEMALE chick is born complete—thousands of ova in her left ovary—and her fate is determined by how well she uses her potential. A good layer can produce an egg a day and is prized for this ability, saved from the fate of her less fertile sisters who will end up in Sunday's roasting pan. Also crucial is the hen's place in the pecking order, a complicated system of queens and hand-maidens set into motion while she is still a pullet and established by the time she is ten weeks old. Luck plays a part, too—which roost the hen happens to be occupying at the moment the keeper's hands move in, setting off a symphony of squawks and screeches and sending feathers swirling to the henhouse ceiling.

Over the summers of my childhood, whenever I visited my grandparents' farm in Indiana, I accompanied Grandma Sylvie on the morning gathering. I was bestowed this honor partly because of my interest but mostly because I was an early riser, unlike Jennifer and Claudia, whose laughter often kept me awake far into their owl nights. I'd wake to the squeak of my grandmother's boots on the stairway. "It's egg time," she'd whisper, and I'd extricate myself from between my sleeping sisters, from the lumpy mattress, its feathers plucked from the bodies of chickens and geese that had ended up in Grandma's oven. I'd dress hurriedly, then follow Grandma downstairs to the kitchen and out the screen door that thudded shut, its springs long since sprung. We'd pass through the garage, past the wringer washer, past the cat and the three-legged dog Mutt curled on the cement floor where oil from Grandpa's truck leaked.

My grandmother was a genius when it came to chickens. She knew how to separate out the potentially good *mothers* from those who were simply good *layers*. She looked for calm birds and passed over any hen with long spurs. "She'd trample the chicks," she'd say. She taught me that leghorns are too flighty, that Rhode Island reds and bantams make the best mothers. But even when you choose carefully, there's still so much that can go wrong: sticky chicks, crippled chicks, chicks that pip but never hatch, chicks born dead in the shell. I didn't like to think about the dead ones. The year before I was born, my mother had a baby girl that died. Mother almost died with her, is the way Aunt Bessie told it. Mother never talked about that time. She lived in the present; the past was something she could put down like knitting. And that particular summer, 1961, she was pregnant again, her stomach so hard and tight that I was afraid it would burst before my father got home from his overseas duty.

Most eggs come from hens that have never seen a rooster; you need a rooster only if you want chicks. According to Grandma, the layers were the most contented of the lot, and the henhouse *did* seem a happy place, row after row of red hens squawking away their noisy roosterless lives. Some sat two to a nest, their heads close together in a duet of chirps and chirrs. A few gave up their eggs blithely, but most screeched and flapped their tail feathers like weapons if you got too near their nests. At first I was timid, afraid of trespassing into the wrong nest and stealing an egg destined for chickness. "How does a hen know?" I asked. Meaning, how does a hen know if the egg she's setting is a chick or a regular breakfast egg. "She doesn't," Grandma said. "When a hen gets broody, it doesn't matter what's under her. Sometimes there's nothing there at all. One banty sat on green apples for weeks."

It didn't take me long to learn the signs of broodiness. A

broody hen was obstinate, uncooperative. She puffed herself up to twice normal size and strutted to the nest where she sat, staring straight ahead, her eyes emptied-out and dreamy. Sometimes an old hen, long past laying, would get broody and try to set the eggs of a younger hen. When this happened, Grandma always left them alone. "She'll hatch them just fine," she said, "and raise a brood better than some giddy pullet. Besides, she's not good for much else." According to Grandma, an old hen was too tough to be a good roaster. But her liver was still tasty, and she made a good stew; her legs made a passable jelly base.

I told my love a story that had no end

GRANDMA had an older sister, a troll of a woman with clattery teeth and big black shoes. Aunt Bessie, who lived at Grandma's farm most of the time, arrived at our house on schedule each time my mother gave birth. She was not particularly good with babies, but she was available. Since she belonged to no one, she could easily pull up stakes and join my mother for as long as we needed her. For years, she bragged to anyone in listening distance that she had soaked her corns in both the Atlantic and the Pacific.

When I was born, my mother already had two small children and had recently buried an infant; she needed all the help she could get. So Bessie stayed on for years, accumulating intimate knowledge I would later consider an unfair advantage. She hoarded all the details, pulling them out for display to anyone who would listen—friends, family, and later, my boyfriends. "She was a little card," she'd say, as she broke into yet another tale about my cowlicks that wouldn't lie straight, my speech impediment (for years I couldn't pronounce 's'), my retardation in the areas of toilet training and bottle feeding. "I thought we'd never get her off the breast!" she'd say. "Why, once I saw her stand up beside Juanita while she was driving—stand up, mind you, in those little patent leather shoes—and work her mouth into Juanita's blouse. While she was driving, no less! Why, we thought we were going to have to send Juanita to school with her!"

"You're her favorite," Mother always said, which made me cringe. I didn't want to be Aunt Bessie's favorite. I didn't like the way she sidled up to me on the couch, the way she leaned forward to repeat yet another story about the child I used to be. It's one thing for a mother to know you too well; an aunt has no right. Yet Bessie knew no such boundaries. She never let me forget that she had practically raised me.

In 1954, when we were stationed in Texas, one morning over breakfast my mother announced that we were going to have a new baby in the house. Tom and Jennifer seemed oblivious to the upcoming event. They'd already started school and seemed to believe there were more important things in the world than the crib my father had unpacked from the storage closet. But I recognized the crib as my own and watched as the white slats were painted yellow, then reassembled and set up in my parents' bedroom. One day Aunt Bessie returned from shopping carrying a cloth doll that she attempted to insinuate into my arms.

When Mother left for the hospital, I was left alone with Aunt Bessie, whose neck lay in great folds like a chicken's wattle. A few days later she told me my mother was coming back from the hospital. She fairly chirped with the news: "You have a sister. Her name is Claudia. We need to get things ready." She took off her big black shoes and put on the fluffy slippers she wore for housework. I dressed myself in cowboy boots, a pair of shorts but no top, and my father's long dark socks which I pulled high over my knees. (I don't remember doing this, but these are the details Bessie later supplied.) Then I went out into the yard to dig a trench with a miniature shovel. After a while Aunt Bessie began backing out of the kitchen with the mop in her hand, covering her tracks. I started walking toward the door.

"Don't go in there with those muddy boots," she said.

I kept walking.

"I've just mopped. Everything's ready for the baby." I stomped to the back porch, past Aunt Bessie who was incapacitated for the moment, her hands deep in a bucket of gray water, wringing the mop. She reached out with one hand, but missed. "I mean it, don't go in there." I opened the screen door, then slammed it in her face. "Come back here, you rascal. You come back here this minute." I remember how good it felt, stomping across the shiny wet floor, digging my heels in hard to make my newly discovered weight felt and heard.

Within a few hours the crib was full, stuffed with a baby girl who had too much hair for her head. Aunt Bessie stood guard, eyeing me suspiciously. I knew the story of Hansel and Gretel, how the witch kept the children in the cage to fatten them up. The new baby seemed to be swelling already, her dimpled skin packed tight. Yet every time I looked, Mother was opening her blouse and putting the baby's mouth there. The baby was fat enough, she didn't need more milk, why did my mother keep doing this?

"Oh, I could just eat you up," my mother would say, chewing on a bit of plump thigh. I'd watch her and think *Keep going. Chew the whole leg off. Bite off the arms, too. And the head while you're at it.*

Once while Aunt Bessie wasn't looking, I had reached through the slats, grabbed hold of a hand, and crammed the whole thing into my mouth, surprised to discover bones beneath the skin. *Be he alive or be he dead, I'll grind his bones to make my bread.* My teeth were white and strong and even. We'd recently had corn on the cob for dinner, and I knew that if I could dismantle a whole roasting ear by myself, I could easily take care of this. But just as I was about to bite, Aunt Bessie careened around the corner in her slippers, sliding to a stop on the freshly polished floor. She grabbed my arm and pulled me away. It was then I realized that the crib wasn't meant to keep the baby in, but to keep me out. It's not that I wanted Claudia dead—the word meant nothing to me yet. I simply wanted her gone. We'd been doing just fine without her.

"Be careful," Mother would say, on the rare occasions when she handed me the baby. "Hold her neck up. Be careful of the soft spot." The soft spot. Of course. I knew the baby's head wasn't finished yet, that it would take a while for the bones to grow together. I stared at the indentation for a long time, watching the pulse beat, beat, beat, beat. But just when the moment was right, Aunt Bessie was there, her bony hands fluttering like birds into my face.

AFTER WE'D GATHERED the eggs, I'd follow Grandma through the field, swinging the basket in time to her steps, hurrying to keep up. Her steps were large and purposeful, and she seemed in that instant simultaneously larger and smaller than herself, bearing the accumulated weight of the stories I'd heard about her, the stories I'd snatched up in my hunger, beheaded, disemboweled, plucked free of mundane factual truth, and basted with the juices of imagination until what was left bore little resemblance to the original squawking reality. By the time we made it back to the farmhouse, the sun was a yellow dazzle on the tin roof and it seemed incomprehensible that everyone in the world should not be halfway through their morning tasks. Yet inside the house, my brothers and sisters were still asleep. Mother too, alone behind the door of the sleeping porch, sprawled across a nest of feather pillows. Only Bessie was up, studying the newspaper obituaries, her first act of each day. The cat snored at her feet. When I came through the door, Bessie's small face caved into a smile. "Good morning, Becky," she said, but since she hadn't put her teeth in yet, my nickname came out muffled, too much like "Bessie." I would start calling myself Rebecca.

With both hands, Grandma lifted the iron skillet from the shelf and set it onto the eye of the wood stove. She opened the metal container filled with bacon grease and rubbed the grease into the skillet. One by one I checked the eggs, rubbing gently with a cloth to loosen any dirt or feces. (You should never wash an egg unless you have to. Water destroys the protective bloom.) When the grease began to sizzle, I reached for the two finest brown eggs, still warm. The shell broke against the side of the skillet and the clear albumin became white, forming a pond around the yolk. The eggs popped and snapped. While Grandma buttered bread to warm in the oven, I took a spatula and spooned grease onto the eggs until the yellow was covered in a smooth whiteness. Then I slid the spatula beneath the eggs—first Grandma's, then mine—and lifted them carefully onto the blue plates.

I gave my love a baby with no crying

"IN THROUGH the nose, out through the mouth. In through the nose, out through the mouth." Holly weaves among us, stepping carefully between pillows and bodies. It's our last Lamaze session. "You're blowing up a balloon, ladies. A big balloon. No hissing, Victoria, relax your teeth. In through the nose, out through the mouth. Coaches, ready with the effleurage." Jim is resting, sitting back on his heels; it's my turn. I sprinkle the powder over Lana's abdomen and place my fingers above her pubic bone, arching my palms high as if preparing to play scales on the piano. I am a butterfly. Brushing lightly, lightly.

"This is a fifty second contraction, ladies. You're at seven centimeters, about the size of a fifty-cent piece. Ready? Begin."

I look into Lana's eyes and take a deep breath. Jim clicks the stopwatch and begins counting. "Five . . . ten . . . twenty . . ." In through the nose, out through the mouth, I'm blowing up a big balloon. "Thirty-five . . . forty." I'm getting dizzy. "Forty-five . . . fifty."

"Rest," Holly says. "Now breathe normally. You will have about four minutes before the next one. Use the time to rest. The next set will last one minute and the contractions will be much stronger. Think of the contraction as a wave. Swim over the top, ladies. Over the wave."

"Surfin' U.S.A.," says Lana. I look over at Jim. He shrugs, smiles a calm half-smile.

"Keep your eye on the wave, ladies. Swim above it. Don't panic or you'll be submerged. Ready? A big greeting breath. Now begin."

When the practice session is over we gather in our final circle, waiting for Holly to join us for closing remarks. We sit cross-legged on the floor like children at a birthday party: boy, girl, boy, girl. Duck, duck, goose. Jim and Lana are on my left; Dirk, the auto parts salesman, on my right. His nails are bitten to the quick. "Did you hear about Stacy?" he says nervously.

Across the circle, Earl looks up. "She's doing fine," he says. Earl is Steve's friend. He was the one who talked Steve and Stacy into the childbirth classes.

"Was it a boy?" Lana says.

Earl looks down at his huge hands, spread across his knees. "A boy," he says, without looking up.

Dirk looks anxiously side to side like a child cheating on a test. There's no sign of Holly. He leans down and, in a stage whisper, delivers the news. "It was stillborn. They knew for five days but she waited it out, can you imagine waiting like that, knowing that it's dead, then finally they induced labor, can you imagine . . ."

Holly enters and silences the salesman with one look. She squeezes in between Earl and his wife, keeping her eye on the salesman as she begins to speak. "Victoria, that was much improved—excellent on the pant-and-blow. Lana, you need to concentrate more during contractions. But overall, I feel totally confident that you are all ready." She takes a deep breath and folds her plump hands across her stomach. "The next few weeks will be full of ups and downs. There will be days when you'll want to sing and dance, when you'll get a burst of energy like you've never known before. You might get an urge to clean the house from top to bottom—I always wanted to paint. Then the next day you'll be so tired you won't be able to lift your head off the bed. One day you'll be starving, the next day the thought of food will make you ill. All of this is normal. You will be fine. Just remember the basics. Rest. Stay relaxed and focused. Breathe. And when the big waves come, swim over them." She lifts a forefinger and wags it in the air. "And I want a birth announcement from everyone. Everyone, Earl! Okay?"

"Miss July," Earl says. "Va-va-voom."

Holly looks around the circle. "I know some of you have been concerned about Stacy. Steve says to tell you she's doing fine. Her mother is here, taking care of things." *Taking care of things.* So much to do—name the child, sign the birth certificate, the death certificate. I wonder what they'll do with the ceiling train.

Holly continues. "I want to reassure you that what happened to Stacy is extremely rare. Birth is a natural process, as natural as eating or breathing or sleeping. Nature takes care of things." Poor Holly: three miscarriages. Nature certainly took care of her. "You're all feeling a little anxious right now, but you must try to stay positive and focused toward your baby."

Earl clears his throat, looks up. "Isn't there something we could do? A card or some flowers?"

"I'm sure they'd appreciate that. The worst thing is not to acknowledge it. That's the way it is, people just ignore it, like it never happened, or they tell you oh, it's for the best, there's a reason, it's nature's way and all that, the baby probably would have suffered, and if you have to lose a child, best to lose him now, you know." Holly's voice is rising, teetering on the edge. The salesman reaches for his wife's hand and Earl rises on one knee as if he might bolt toward Holly. Then suddenly she stops, closes her eyes, and takes a deep cleansing breath. "Yes, a card would be nice. What a nice idea, Earl. I'm sure Stacy would appreciate a card."

THE HARDEST THING on earth to bear is the death of a child. That's what all the books say. But books are written by grownups. As a child, I could imagine nothing worse than one of my parents dying. If one of them died, I'd have to start from scratch, inventing a new life. My parents, on the other hand, had had other lives before me. I'd seen the pictures. Mother was a girl once, a teenager, a young woman, even a wife, without one day missing me. Yet from my first breath, there she was. To speak, in the same breath, *death* and *mother* would have been impossible. Death didn't lurk in the waffle batter, in the reflection of newly waxed linoleum, or in my mother's maternity blouses flapping on the clothesline. *Mother* was synonymous with life. Under her touch, everything bloomed. Cakes rose high and magnificent, roses opened with a sprinkle from her watering can, flat fabric passing through the jaws of her sewing machine emerged on the other side as three-dimensional dresses with Peter Pan collars and puffy sleeves. And, most stunning of all, she could grow babies.

The secrets of the body had always fascinated me. Even before I could read, I'd spend hours studying the transparent overlays in *Encyclopædia Britannica*. It seemed a miracle, the way all the systems fit together—digestive and circulatory and reproductive. Even the colors in the transparencies matched, giving me a patriotic feeling, all that red and blue swirling together. Later on I loved the film the Girl Scout leader showed, especially the part where a pink egg sets out, like a tiny explorer ship, on its slow-motion voyage through the fallopian tubes. And through it all there was my mother, a great ship set sail. I loved the globelike roundness beneath her muumuu and the awkward way she backed into chairs. Sometimes I would stand before the bathroom mirror with a pillow stuffed under my pajama top, turning sideways to admire the bulge. But unlike most little girls who play Mommy, I had witnessed the mystery beneath the muumuu.

I still recall everything about the moment, down to the smell of chlorine and suntan oil. I was five years old, Claudia was not yet one, and Mother was pregnant with Rick, her fifth living child.

She had driven us to the pool at the base, and I was in the dressing room beside her, holding my little sister Claudia. Mother had removed her maternity smock and folded it on the wooden bench, beside the red cotton romper she used as a swimsuit. When she unhooked her bra (she called it a brassiere), her breasts fell loose and heavy. Stretch marks that began in the cave of her armpits rippled down her sides. She moved her hands to the cotton panties that were pulled high over the top of her belly, and when she stepped out of the panties, I saw the belly—huge and white, capped by a navel round as a cherry. Somewhere beneath all that whiteness, I thought, is a baby. I couldn't stop staring. It was as if the whole universe was suspended between us. I could not have known, in that moment, that the universe had already begun to shift. At first the movement was nearly imperceptible—a planet here, a planet there, the small events of my life lining up. It would take seven years for the stars to fully align themselves, but by the end of my twelfth summer, my world would be eclipsed.

How can there be a cherry that has no stone?

ABOVE our heads, the oars of a ceiling fan paddled the heat. It was 1961, and I was sitting at the oilcloth-covered table with Mother and Grandma, pitting cherries and thinking about Sylvia's grave. The day before, we'd driven over the border into Illinois, where my infant sister was buried. Mother slid the bucket of cherries to the center of the table. One large vein was pulsing on her hand. Before the trip to the cemetery, I'd aligned my mother with the Indian squaws I'd read about in *National Geographic,* the ones who squatted in the field, dislodged their babies (as painlessly as bowel movements, I imagined), and within minutes went back to their hoes and spades. Mother's hair was thick and black as an Indian's, but a faint gray streak was visible at the crown.

She sighed and leaned forward, readjusting her belly. Mother seemed always just about to say something, and I kept hoping that if I waited long enough, the words would come. Aunt Bessie was sitting on the foldout couch that would become her bed that night. She stroked the cat's back with one hand and held a newspaper in the other as she recited yesterday's soybean prices. It was the last day of our visit, and the cycle was as predictable as the moon. Tomorrow we would leave for the long drive home—this time to Virginia, three states away—and of course Aunt Bessie would go with us.

Grandma Sylvie was the quickest pitter. Already her fingertips were blackened with juice; she could pit a whole bowlful without looking. My pitting method was more surgical than culinary. I was both prim and barbaric, avoiding the inevitable moment of plunging into the fruit to search for the stone, yet, in the process, worrying the cherries so much that they ended up bruised and battered when I finally dropped them into the bowl. Two months shy of my twelfth birthday, I hadn't yet heard the word *cherry* uttered as a schoolyard smirk. I didn't know it was something a girl could give a boy. Boys existed only peripherally, at the edges of my world. Sometimes they showed up on our doorstep looking for my brothers, sometimes for my older sister Jennifer. I'd seen their Adam's apples bobbing and heard their tentative voices break in the middle of a word.

I reached for another handful of cherries. They were plump and slick, so ripe they were nearly black. Grandma looked at my bowl and shook her head. It was indeed a miserable showing, less than a dozen cherries. How would I ever get enough for a pie? On the tree they looked so large, it seemed a simple nursery rhyme task to transform them into pies—four-and-twenty blackbirds. But as I stared into my bowl, I saw that it would take many cherries, a hundred or more, to make one pie. By the time they were washed, stemmed, pitted, sugared, floured, and baked, they would have shrunk to a third their size. This seemed a waste to me, like so much of what my mother did each day—making beds in the morning, cooking breakfast, washing dishes, fixing lunch, washing dishes, cooking dinner, washing dishes, turning down the beds at night, fluffing the pillows minutes before we would flatten them, leaving the imprints of our heads.

Mother's thumb hesitated an instant inside the fruit, as if reluctant to let the stone go. Her gaze wandered out the window. Was she missing my father? Was she thinking about the grave? She rolled the stone between her fingers as if caressing it, before releasing it into the pile. Then she brushed back her hair with the flat of her hand, leaving a stain on her temple. Grandma grabbed a cherry and yanked off the stem, slit the cherry with a thumbnail filed needle-sharp for this purpose, popped out the stone, and tossed the cherry into the earthenware bowl, all in one swift movement. Her hands were sprinkled with age, the skin rough and cracked like dried-up clay, the knuckles so knotted it was as if she had outgrown her skin and the bones were trying to push through. A wisp of hair had escaped my mother's headband and now fluttered upwards toward the fan. The minutes wore on. Aunt Bessie kept reading, the cat began to snore softly, and with each orbit of the ceiling fan the room grew warmer. My fingertips were waterlogged and shriveled. Yesterday the cat had scratched my hand, drawing blood, and the acid in the cherries reawakened the sting.

How can there be a chicken that has no bone?

WHEN I WALK INTO our bedroom after the last Lamaze class, Donald is in bed reading. He has filled Aunt Bessie's clay vase—the one she gave me years ago—with fresh flowers. As I undress, I try to describe the film Holly showed. "I've never seen anything like it . . . when you see the head . . . when it crowns . . ." My throat is thick with what could easily become tears. Donald takes off his reading glasses and lays the magazine face-down on the quilt. The light from the lamp accents his chest, salted with gray hairs. "Are you sure this is a good idea?"

"Lana asked me, remember?"

"Don't get defensive."

"I'm not defensive." I climb under the sheet.

"All I asked is are you sure it's a good idea."

"I'm over that." The past year had been a bleak one. I'd find myself crying for no reason, hours at a stretch. Some mornings I could conjure no reason to get out of bed. I missed three weeks of school—I just couldn't bear to look at all those children.

"Maybe you should give Bob a call," Donald says.

"His name is Bill."

"Bill."

"He'll just say the same old thing. Or not say it. Sometimes he'd just sit there and nod. Eighty dollars an hour to say nothing." I plump my pillow into shape. "Did you know that if you leave a space in the middle of 'therapist,' it spells 'the rapist'?"

"What about Philistine What's-Her-Name? I thought you liked her."

"Philistine wears Birkenstocks. *Birkenstocks,* for God's sake. I saw her in the grocery store and she told me about her new workshop. *Empowerment!* If I hear that word one more time, I'll scream. She had on this wrinkled tent thing. She's pregnant again. That's all I need, an Earth Mother therapist."

"Rapist," Donald says, laying his glasses on the nightstand.

"She's got African fertility goddesses all over her bookshelves. She doesn't shave her armpits."

"Your logic never ceases to amaze me." Donald rubs the bridge of his nose where his glasses have left tiny red dents. Without glasses, he looks older, more exposed to the elements of time. In the past few years gravity has begun its work, tugging at the edges of the blue eyes that now slant downward like the eyes of a sad puppy. He switches off the reading light and moves toward me, curling his leg over mine. His legs are slim and finely muscled, the legs of a much younger man.

"Maybe we were too hasty," he says. "If I'd ever thought you'd change your mind . . ." He places his hands on my breasts, plumped from the estrogen I've been taking this past year. Menopause is a strange word. You can break it into so many pieces.

"It's ancient history," I say. "We had our reasons." And I was the one who insisted, I think. I made the appointment with the urologist, I brought the ice packs to the bed. It was for the best, we believed—a mutual decision, well thought out and perfectly executed. And now, sixteen years later, it makes no sense. I know what all the books say, that what I'm feeling, what I'm hearing, is my tightly wound biological clock. But when I put my ear to the task, I hear no ticking, no heartbeat, no animal thump. What I hear is a word: *Motherhood, Motherhood.* An Indian drum beat, a chant over a firelit circle of women. Then the word breaks apart like an ember, and an image rises smokelike above the circle: *Mother Hood. Mother Hood.* A cloak to slip over my shoulders when the nights get too chilly. A heavy cloak, scratchy against my skin.

I turn to lie on my back. A woman on her back could be a girl. Your breasts flatten, fall away from the rib cage. Your stomach hollows out; hipbones emerge. As a child, I never doubted I'd be a mother someday. The children would emerge, freshly scrubbed as the characters in my favorite books. There would be four, two of each, and they would sleep seamlessly down the hall from the master suite I shared with some vague, handsome husband. The future would unfold as naturally as a flower, or a spiral staircase unwinding one carpeted step at a time. It all happened so fast, a few awkward steps, then the accompanying scuffs and bruises, the bloody knees, the scabbing-over and healing, the unexpected slide down the banister into the present. I have been married eighteen years. I have twelve nephews and nieces and am expecting another in a few weeks.

Donald snuffles and sighs, burrowing into his pillow. He isn't gone yet, but in a moment he will be.

"My mother," I whisper, "always won the orchid corsage at church. Every Mother's Day, for having the most children present." Donald's breathing changes; I know he's heard me. "I wasn't good to my dolls." The bedsprings creak, but still he says nothing. "I wasn't mean, exactly."

When he finally speaks, his voice is groggy, the words labored, and I feel a twinge of guilt at disturbing him. "What exactly did you do? Dissect them? Stick pins in their eyes? Torture them?"

"I took care of them whenever I was in the mood, but as soon as something else happened—a friend would come by, or Mom would call us to the table—I'd forget about them. I'd leave them outside. When it rained their bodies would get all spongy. Or the puppy would get to them and tear out the stuffing. I didn't mean any harm, I just had other things to do."

"Sounds like simple neglect to me, not full-fledged abuse. That'll be eighty dollars."

"Lana doesn't look good," I say.

"Don't get started on that again. Try to get some sleep." The streetlight slanting through the miniblinds illuminates the brass edges of the ceiling fan that spins its endless circle. Outside our window, a car alarm begins to throb. To calm myself, I think of the farm—the crooked outhouse silent and dumb; the white fence stretching from the garden to the wooden lean-to; the twin barns edging the inner yard. I think of the horses leaning against the stalls, the steers on their smooth black sides in the straw, Mutt curled on the floor of the musty garage. Somewhere a branch is bending down, releasing its ripe fruit.

How can there be a story that has no end?

THAT SUMMER OF 1961, Aunt Bessie moved into my room, my father returned from overseas, and Vacation Bible School started. The moon made it through another cycle. The predicted date of the baby's birth came and went. Smudges appeared beneath my mother's eyes, and her skin began to pale, despite a surface sheen of perspiration that temporarily flushed her cheeks. Each morning she whirled from the bedroom in a yellow caftan with covered snaps, spinning like a gyroscope or one of those dust devils that whip through the desert. She cleaned closets, brushed cobwebs from the ceiling, stripped wallpaper from the bathroom, and took long walks every night while the rest of us lay in front of the television, exhausted by the swirl of her desperate orbit.

Early one morning while it was still dark, I woke to my father leaning over my bed, whispering to Aunt Bessie, "It's time, I'm taking her." I'd never seen Bessie move so fast. She was out of bed and into her dentures before I had a chance to say good-bye to my father. When I heard his feet hurrying down the stairs and out the back door, I scooted to the edge of the bed and lifted a slat of the venetian blind. The station wagon was in the driveway, gray clouds of exhaust puffing from the tailpipes. My father opened the car door and the interior light switched on. Mother was lying in the back seat. In one brief illumination, I saw the yellow caftan and the black hair. Then my father closed the car door and she disappeared.

THE HOSPITAL kept her longer than usual—*complications* was the word I heard—but soon she was home, looking paler than ever and carrying a very wrinkled, very alive baby she had named Lana. My brother said she looked like Edward G. Robinson and already had dishwater hands, but I liked her big black eyes. My mother relinquished Lana to the bassinet and placed a huge box of white pads beneath the bathroom sink. Enough pads for a year of periods, I thought, yet almost immediately the box began to empty. Each time I went into the bathroom, I checked. Another three or four would be gone. The smudges beneath my mother's eyes darkened, and within a few days she was back in bed wearing a new pink nightgown my father had bought at the PX.

The mews from Lana's mouth weren't full-fledged cries, but they were frequent and irritating, and only my mother's breast could quiet them. "Can't she take a bottle?" I said. Every three hours, when the mews began again, my father or I would carry the baby into their room. Mother would stir from sleep, prop herself against the padded headboard and, with much effort, hold out her arms to accept the baby. Then after some jostling and rooting, when the pink mouth finally fastened onto its target, Mother's head would drop back onto the pillows, and immediately her eyes would close. I thought of Grandma's cat, how the kittens used her, crawling over her body and nudging each other out of the way to claim a nipple. She had always seemed too frail to be a mother cat, and the longer the kittens nursed, the frailer she became, lying trancelike on her side, her black paws stretched before her. Sometimes my mother's eyelids would twitch and I'd know she'd fallen asleep, but not for long, for just then Lana's mouth would pull away, making a popping sound. Time to switch to the other nipple, which was already leaking its thin white liquid onto the rumpled sheet.

Late one night the sound of running water woke me. Beside me Aunt Bessie was snoring. My eyes were gritty with sleep, but when I finally forced them open, I saw a stream of light beneath the bathroom door. Somehow my feet got me there, and when I opened the door I saw my father kneeling over the bathtub. His back was to me and he was wearing his summer khakis, fully dressed except for shoes and socks. The white soles of his feet faced the ceiling. The water was running full strength. He was sloshing something up and down—it made a slapping sound as it hit against the sides of the tub, then a sucking sound as he lifted it from the water. It was my mother's pink nightgown. The water surrounding it was even pinker.

Within a few hours my mother was back in the hospital and

Aunt Bessie was at the kitchen sink pouring formula into a baby bottle. "You're up early," Bessie said when she saw me. Lana was strapped into a carrier propped on the counter, her black eyes glistening with anger. Her mouth opened and the mews began. Bessie took a pair of tongs and lifted a rubber nipple from the pan of boiling water, as if preparing for surgery. What does she know about babies? I thought. I can take care of things.

I shook a rattle before Lana's eyes. "She'll never take a bottle," I said. Bessie unfastened the carrier strap and lifted Lana to her shoulder. "Watch her head," I said. "You have to hold her head."

"Would you hand me the bottle?"

I took the bottle from the counter, held it upside down, and shook it. A few drops of milk dribbled across my wrist. Yes, it was warm enough. "She'll just spit it out," I said as I thrust the bottle toward her.

Bessie settled into my mother's rocker and Lana began mewing again. The mews turned to bleats and her mouth began to quiver. But when Bessie pressed the baby to her, Lana immediately quieted, rooting in the folds of Bessie's blouse. Good luck, I thought. There's no breakfast there. Then Bessie put the bottle to the baby's mouth and squeezed a few drops onto her lips. Lana's mouth seized onto the nipple, sucking so violently that the bottle began to squeak.

"She's sucking in air," I said. This time Bessie looked up. Her mouth was set tight and I knew she wanted to let me have it. Go ahead, I thought. You're not my mother. Just try it. "We don't need you," I said.

Bessie's soft answer startled me. "Would you like to burp her?"

"Burp her yourself. I've got to get ready for Bible School."

I NEVER got to Bible School. I got no farther than my parents'
bedroom, where I found a bundle of bloodied sheets stuffed behind the door. I closed the door and lay on top of the chenille
spread that had been hurriedly flung across the mattress. One by
one my sisters and brothers moved down the stairs to breakfast. I
heard their muffled voices and the periodic thunk of the toaster
releasing slice after slice. I don't know how much my brothers
and sisters knew. Bessie must have told them I was sick—I would
never have gotten away with staying home. The smell of burnt
toast rose up the stairs. Then doors were slamming, footsteps hurrying down the sidewalk.

Hours later I woke face-down on the bed, exhausted. My
throat was raw from crying, and each intake of breath stung my
lungs. Bessie was sitting on the edge of the bed. She ran her hand
down the side of my cheek where the bedspread had carved a
chenille design. "Nice tattoo," she said. "I brought you some tomato soup." Too weak to refuse, I accepted the mug and sipped
the lukewarm soup with saltines crumbled on top—the way my
mother always fixed it. I slurped it down and handed the empty
mug to her.

"Is she dying?" I said. Bessie looked down into the mug. I
twisted the bedspread tighter. "She's dying, isn't she?" It's the
kind of question you ask when you don't really want an answer.
Something makes you say it.

Bessie set the mug down on the table. She took off her glasses
and put them in her pocket. Why is she doing this, I wondered.
She took my face in her hands and lifted my chin, forcing me to
look into her eyes, dark sockets that loomed huge and black
without the softening frame of the glasses. "I don't know," she
said. A piece of the earth broke off and floated away. Then her

arms were around me and I had no choice but to fall into her, into the sagging breasts and the old-flower scent of talcum and age.

How can there be a baby with no crying?

AS IT TURNED OUT, the baby crying in the bassinet, the blood in the bathtub and on the bundled sheets, did not spell the end. Mother came home a week later, and life with its clumsy hands picked us up where it had dropped us. Aunt Bessie seemed lost for a while; then she renewed her assault on the linoleum floors. Baby Lana, returned to my mother's breast, stopped crying and slept through the night. Each day, a wrinkle smoothed out. She began to grow into her eyes. My father said Lana was the most beautiful baby ever, and we let him say it because it was true. After her bath, whenever I could wrestle her away from Aunt Bessie, I'd rub Lana's chest with Johnson's Baby Oil, feeling the indentation between her ribs and the iambic ta-dum ta-dum of her heart, which seemed the smallest yet most profound miracle of all. There was no way I could have suspected—no pediatrician ever did—that Lana was carrying in her chest the same heart that had failed Sylvia. Beneath the pink skin, untouched as yet by sun or wind or any of the world's dangers, was a glitch in the machinery, a mitral valve sputtering. Already the heart was murmuring its secret, but no one would hear it, not for many years.

EXCEPT for the head crowning, nothing is like the film. Lana's labor lasts nineteen hours, and each nurse is surlier than the one before. Everyone's breath is bad. "Get out of my face!" Lana screams when I try to massage her brow. Her black hair is wet with sweat, and it's nearly three A.M. when she finally shifts into transition. "Ride the wave," I say when her jaw begins to tighten.

"You ride it!" she hisses.

Jim begins the effleurage, light stroking movements. "Don't touch me!" she snarls between clenched teeth. "I hate you. This was a bad idea, a really bad idea." The reference is vague enough to allow for interpretation: Lamaze, a bad idea? A vaginal birth? Maybe getting married was the problem. Being a woman seemed to be at the heart of it.

"They say anything," says the tall nurse dryly, rolling her eyes at Jim. "Every woman thinks she's the first to ever have a baby." Lana's legs are shaking, her teeth rattling uncontrollably. "It's killing me!" she screams. "This damned baby is killing me!" The nurse checks the monitor, makes another mark on the chart. Lana's cheeks are flushed with blood, her black eyes shiny as vinyl. Jim leans down into her face. "You're at ten," he whispers. "It's time to push."

When the baby finally slides out, a great wave breaks, water gushing from the table onto the floor. I feel my knees dissolving beneath me, a dizziness in my head, and when I open my eyes, the tall nurse is suctioning out the baby's mouth. He's all head and genitals, his body blue, a slick weasel-sack of skin and blood and hair trembling among the steel bowls and instruments. He bleats. The doctor hands Jim the scissors. The cord is thick and slippery, braided with blood, and it takes both of Jim's carpenter hands to cut it. Lana is sobbing and laughing, her shoulders convulsing with hiccups of joy. Jim places the baby on her breast. The tiny eyelids are squeezed tight, the brow wrinkled in what looks like rage. I brush the hair back from Lana's face and kiss her sweaty forehead. "Look!" she gasps. "Look at all that black hair." My legs are turning to liquid again.

"Jesse," I say. Hot tears are swelling at the edges of my eyes. "He's alive. We got our boy." I reach to touch the top of Jesse's head, but my hand slides off, resting on Lana's soft belly, the accordion pleats of white flesh.

A *cherry when it's blooming, it has no stone*

THE DAY after Lana is released from the hospital, Jim phones, asking me to stop by the pharmacy and pick up a pain prescription for her. "And get something for Jesse," he says. "He's got the colic." When I walk into the bedroom, Jesse is squalling in the bassinet and Lana is sunk into the cave of the waterbed, one hand over her face, the other flopped across the sheet. The gown is open, her breasts engorged. "Want me to bring you the baby?" I say.

She groans and rolls deeper into the waves.

Jim comes in and lifts her head while I give her the pills and water. Lana sinks back into the covers, the waterbed rippling beneath her. I carry Jesse to her, and Jim arranges three pillows against the headboard. "Here's the little guy," he says. Lana groans again and Jim's voice turns stern, scolding. "Wake up, Lana. The baby needs to eat."

Lana stirs, but does not open her eyes. Jim puts the baby to her breast and Jesse quiets, begins to suck. Lana's arms flop loose again. "Take him away," she says flatly, and turns to fall back into the covers, unhooking the baby's mouth from her nipple. Milk dribbles onto the sheet.

I pick up Jesse and follow Jim into the kitchen. A dried-out sandwich lies on the counter beside an overturned cup of apple juice. "Where's Hanah?" I say.

"I finally got her to sleep."

"How long has Lana been like this? It smells like something died in there."

"She'll be fine," he snaps. His pale blue eyes are rimmed with red. "It's just a bad headache. Once the medicine kicks in—"

"Jim!" The wail is high-pitched, desperate, the unearthly cry of an animal caught in a trap. Jim bolts toward the hallway and I follow with Jesse on my shoulder. When I turn the corner into the bedroom, Lana is sitting up, her head lolling on her shoulders, the dark eyes fixed and unblinking. She's clawing the air with her hands. "I can't see! I can't see!"

Jim climbs onto the waterbed and crawls toward her. He waves his hands in front of her eyes. "Call the hospital, Becky. Lana, it's me. Here's my arm. Come on, let's get you into your robe." Jesse starts to cry. I shift him from my shoulder to the crook of my arm and begin to bounce him softly. "I said, call the hospital!"

I find the number quickly. My fingers punch the code as if they've been programmed in advance. I feel unhurried, calm, amazed at how well I can manage with one hand. Jesse has stopped crying. When I hang up the phone, I feel quieted and slightly bored, as if I'm watching a television show I've seen before and can turn the channel whenever I choose. "They're waiting," I say. "They'll have a gurney ready, and a specialist."

Jim has scooped Lana into his arms and is bounding toward the door. I open it with one hand and stand aside. "Stay with the babies," Jim says. "I'll call you from the emergency room."

"Do you know how to get to the hospital? I could drive you,"

I say. But he is out the front door and halfway down the steps when Hanah appears, dragging a shred of yellow security blanket. Jesse wakes and begins to cry. I cradle him close, slide my little finger into his mouth, and feel the wet hard gums begin their work.

And a chicken 'fore its pipping, it has no bone

CRISIS has always had an invigorating effect on my mother, like a splash from a mountain stream. For three days she's been shuttling between house and hospital, sleeping only a few hours at a time, yet in this dim light I can't see the lines around her eyes or the fine drapery of wrinkles on her neck. She looks surprisingly young, like those girls in high school yearbooks, the ones who were always going steady. She's wearing the car keys on a long chain around her neck.

"Who's with her now?" I ask. "Claudia?"

Mother nods. She won't leave Lana's bedside unless someone is there. Years ago, she lost Aunt Bessie between shifts. She'd left for a few minutes, just long enough to get a cup of coffee, and when she got back, the EKG line was flat. After all the watching, the midnight vigils, when the moment finally came my great-aunt died alone. Mother grabs a piece of toast and heads down the hall toward the bathroom. She won't be long—a quick marine bath, as she calls it. Just the three f's—face, feet, fanny. No time for makeup or elaborate hair styling. She'll simply comb her thick hair straight back and secure it with a headband: the two-minute miracle, my father calls her.

She appears in the doorway, smelling of Ivory soap. "Are you sure you don't want to go?" she says. I shake my head. She swipes

Chap Stick across her lips and turns to leave, the car keys jangling against her shirt.

SEPTIC EMBOLI. Acute endocarditis. Optic nerve. Electrocardiograph. Brain scan. Mitral valve. The words become my anchors, providing weight and purpose to my days. I write them on notepads, memorize them, repeat them into the receiver each time another relative or friend calls—Jennifer from California, my brother from Idaho, Lana's neighbors, church friends of my parents I haven't seen in decades. By the second week I have it down. I'm a prerecorded message, a sixty-second sound bite: "She contracted an infection." It's always *she*. This is a generic patient we're talking about. To speak her name would unlock Rumpelstiltskin's secret, wrest from Jacob's angel the magical power. "Bacteria is always present during delivery, but usually it passes out of the body. Hers didn't. It shot up to the optic nerve and blinded her. Yes, she has her sight back, but it's blurry and there are wedges missing, like pieces of a pie. Then it settled in her heart—she had a bad valve all along. No, no one knew. Penicillin: five hundred thousand units a day, directly into her heart."

Over the next week Mother and Jim and Claudia take turns trying to sleep in the plastic chairs in intensive care. Every few hours one of them calls with an update. "The IC nurses are angels," Mother keeps saying, and I think yes, that's why their shoes are so padded and soft. They're not nurses at all. They're boneless, weightless. Their white stockings are bubbles of air. That's how they float in and out of the room so quietly, easing the relatives into a sphere of soundlessness, preparation for the final winged visitation.

Which I want nothing to do with. Give me lists and screaming babies. Anything but silence, those desert spaces where you wait—for the minute hand to jump, the IV to drip, the dark eyes to flutter open then shut again. I'll take the colicky Jesse, his shaky bleats, the mustard-filled diapers, the sour burp rags on my shoulder. Give me Hanah with her tugs and tantrums, her pouty lips: "Where's Mommy? I hate you, go away. Where's my Mommy?" Here, dirty dishes pile up at my elbows. There are grocery lists to make, ringing phones to answer, the comforting slosh of the washing machine, the *eek! eek!* of the dryer belt rubbing itself raw from usefulness. There's orange juice to sponge off car seats and cracker crumbs leaping from the lip of the dustpan. Everything swirling, burping, screaming, beeping, each creaking hour a cog in the wheel. Days I am dizzy with activity, and nights, dazed with exhaustion, I hunger for more musts and have-tos. When I stop, it's too quiet. I rush to Jesse's crib, touch his chest, put my ear to his mouth, awaiting his next breath. In the silence I wind the farmyard mobile and watch it turn, watch the chickens and geese and cows bounce vacantly on their strings, following each other blindly around and around the circle, going nowhere, but going fast.

The story of I Love You, it has no end

IN the corner of the room Mother is rocking Jesse. She's wearing a calico tent dress, and each backward tilt of her body momentarily obscures the light from the lamp behind her head. Rock up, rock back, the light on, now off, on, off, the movement of the rocker even and sure, an optical rhythm strobing the room into an old-time movie. I am lying beside Hanah in Lana's waterbed.

"I must have fallen asleep," I say.

"Look, the baby turned his head," she says. "He knows your

voice already." Rock up, rock back, light on, off. Jesse sucks on the bottle—squeak, squeak. She tosses the burp rag onto her shoulder, lifts Jesse, and begins to pat. Up, back, up, back. The waterbed dips and splashes beneath me—Hanah must be dreaming. Her head is sweaty, the fine blond hair streaked with saliva. Today when Mother took her to intensive care, Hanah kicked the hospital bed and tried to yank out the IV, and since then, she won't let me out of her sight. Even in sleep, she reaches for me.

The rocker stops. Mother spreads the blanket across her lap, tucks Jesse's arms close to his sides, and winds the blanket around him like a mummy's wrappings. "Indians did this to keep the babies quiet during attacks," she says. "It calms them." Mother turns the papoose onto his stomach, begins to pat his back. "We need to make plans," she says. "Have you thought about a plan?"

I close my eyes against the question.

"Even if she makes it, she might not be the same," she says. The rocker starts up again. "Lana was a beautiful child."

"Everyone's favorite."

"I have no favorites," Mother says.

"What did the doctor say? I thought she was stable. The odds are better now, aren't they?"

"Parents should not outlive their children," she says to the air.

"Each day the odds are better, right?"

Mother stares at the wall as if reading a cave message painted there. Each word she speaks is a discovery. "Twelve more hours and she would have been gone. It's a blessing she lost her sight. Otherwise we might not have known." She turns to me; the message on the wall must have run out. "Have you talked to Jim? Does he have a plan?"

"You know Jim—everything's under control. He won't talk."

"There are two babies here. I've got my dad to take care of."

"School doesn't start for another month."

"Two babies. Claudia's got her hands full. Jennifer too."

"I might be able to take a leave of absence, a couple of months even."

The rocker stops. Mother closes her eyes, pulls the papoose to her breast. Her voice is a thin fabric wrung out to dry. "I'm talking about the rest of your life." In the kitchen the ice maker purrs, pauses, clanks into a new rhythm. The cubes drop into their preordained places.

IN MY DREAM we are at the farm again. Mother is barefoot in the garage, standing over the wringer washer. She's wearing the calico tent dress. The dashers rock, beating the clothing, bits of color surfacing here and there among the suds. She's staring into the washer as if she's lost something but can't remember what it is, or hasn't the energy to retrieve it. The air is moist, thick with the smell of detergent and dog. Mutt is sprawled beneath the legs of the washer, which bumps and knocks against the wet cement floor. Loose bubbles and suds float down onto his fur.

Mother flips the switch. The rollers clamp together and begin to turn. I slip my hands into the tub and reach for a knot of yellow—Mother's caftan of thirty years ago. I ease it toward the rollers. "Watch your fingers," Mother says automatically, like a telephone recording. I feel the tug as the caftan is pulled from my hands and through the rollers. The next piece is Lana's blue hospital gown. I untangle it from Mother's pink nightgown. One by one I separate the pieces of clothing and feed them to the waiting rollers, which suck them through and squeeze them nearly dry before the clothes land in the tub of clean water on the other side.

And a baby when it's sleeping, there's no crying

WHEN I was small I used to lie in bed and worry about cells. I would tongue the vacant space in my mouth, wondering how my body would know to grow a new tooth there. I rubbed the paper cut on my finger. How did it know? Of all the possible things that could grow from the wound, why new finger cells? What would keep my body from misfiring, sprouting on my fingertip a white molar or an eyebrow or toenail?

"It just knows," my mother would say. "Things work out. The body knows." Years later a dentist removed my wisdom teeth and left, in their place, magic stitches. "They'll dissolve on their own," he said. "You won't even know when it happens." That's the way it was for my mother. One morning, she says, months after Sylvia's death, she woke and the sky looked different. Part of it was hers again, that big blue hunk above the tomato patch. Where had she gone all those months? What disembodied hand had fed her children, patted them to sleep? Yet here they were in their beds, whole. And the new one in her belly—welcome, welcome. The laundry was swelling on the line, puffed up with spring wind. That night when my father reached for her, she recognized his touch. The stone rolled away from the door.

LANA is sitting in the rocker, nursing Jesse. His hair is a black nest against the whiteness of her breast. Last week the surgeon removed the catheter from her heart, and only a small red dent remains to mark the wound. My bags are packed and waiting by the door. In the next room, Hanah is supposed to be napping, but I can hear her feet thumping against the wall. Lana closes one eye and stares at me. "You're disappearing again," she says. "You're floating behind my eye." The visual disturbances are less frequent now, less severe. In another few months, according to the doctors, her sight will be fully restored. When that time comes, she says, the first thing she's going to do is get her camera down from the shelf. She says that the world is brighter than she'd remembered it, the outlines more defined.

I walk to Hanah's room and lie down beside her on the narrow bed. Jim has painted stars and a pockmarked moon on the dark blue ceiling. They glow phosphorescent; the stars seem to blink. In the corner, high above our heads, hangs a hammock filled with stuffed animals and dolls. I lie still for a long time, staring at the painted sky and waiting for Hanah's breathing to change. My eyes grow heavier each minute. The world is all wrong—grown-ups are exhausted, and kids get all the naps. I hear the crush of Pampers as she turns. After a few minutes her breathing begins to change. First, shallow puffs. Then long slow strokes like the rise and dip of oars, the paddles dipping in and out, in and out, submerging then surfacing, submerging again as she enters what I imagine to be a deep turquoise sleep. Suddenly she snuffles, mumbles something I can't make out; the muscles in her back twitch. What is she dreaming? I rub my hand across her back to calm her, and within seconds her breathing smooths out again. I take a deep breath and row out behind her.

THERE IS no crayon the color of this vase. It would take the mixing of many palettes—blue-green seas you have imagined but never seen, tinged with ocher mud and sherry swirled in crystal goblets. When Aunt Bessie gave me the vase for high school graduation, she told me the clay was born this color. "There's none like it anywhere on earth," she said. That's what the Indian had told her. She'd bought the vase at a trading post during the early sixties, on one of her many bus trips out West to visit us. "So the vase is precious," she said, as she handed it to me. "I saved it for you, for a special occasion. You're as close to a daughter as I'll ever have."

One day years later when I was visiting my parents, Bessie suddenly looked up from the dinner table and said, "You never thanked me for that vase." My parents had recently moved Bessie into the spare bedroom where all her possessions, which had once filled the attic at the farm, had been packed into a mahogany chest. "It wouldn't have taken much," she said, her chin trembling with emotion. "But you never thanked me."

"Of course I did," I said. My mother nodded in agreement. I remembered writing the card and putting it in her suitcase on our way to the bus station. Bessie shook her head, which seemed too large for her doll-like body. "A little gratitude, that's all I expected," she said. "It was so precious. No clay like it anywhere."

And over and over, throughout the remaining years of her life, whenever she saw me, the subject of the vase would come up, the same old record stuck in the same old groove. It was as if all our time together, all those years, had shrunk to a space small enough to hold a bouquet. "Five minutes," she'd say. "That's all it would have taken. A simple thank-you. I should have given it to someone else. Someone who'd appreciate it."

For thirty years I have used it at my table, filled it with daffodils in March, summer wildflowers, evergreen and holly at Christmas. I love the rough feel of it, the rounded curves. The hourglass figure fits perfectly into the scoop of my hands. It doesn't matter that last week while I was cleaning the vase, a smear of blue-green stain rubbed off onto the towel, exposing the clay beneath. Plain brown clay. Ordinary as the ground from which it was dug, ordinary as hundreds of others cast from the same mold. And no vase like it, anywhere on earth.

the cloud's immaculate folds

WHEN the water broke, Jennifer turned from my mother's stove where she was stirring a pot of spaghetti, her cheeks flushed from steam and pregnancy. The look on her face was stunned—brown eyes wide, mouth open—as she stared across the kitchen table where I was arranging the dinner plates. She was wearing a maternity dress she'd made herself, a sleeveless blue calico with a white collar. She dropped the spoon and looked down at her feet, where a puddle had formed. She stared for a few seconds, then looked back at me, her eyes almost comical in surprise. Incredulous.

"Your water broke," I said. "It's time." I knew she knew this. She was, after all, my *older* sister, twenty-three and married, and she'd been reading the books for months, but apparently none of it had sunk in. Although Jennifer was smart, a good reader, she did not believe in books the way I did. She did not live *inside* them. If quizzed, she could recite all the facts, but none of them seemed to touch her. In this way, and in others, she remained immaculately innocent. Everything was news to Jennifer. Even this—the dam breaking and nowhere to run.

Thirty years later, the moment remains in memory—the steam in the kitchen, her stunned face turning to me, the way she bit her bottom lip as if to say *I've wet myself, what a childish thing to do, and me with these breasts and this belly.* Did I cross the room and put my arms around her? I remember wanting to, feeling the need to shield her from something, though I didn't know what. I wanted everything to go back, years back; how had we gotten here so soon? The feeling lasted a few seconds, then my mother appeared to rush my sister to the bathroom and my father was on the phone trying to track down Jennifer's husband.

WHEN I WAS YOUNG, for many years I assumed I was the eldest daughter. The fact that Jennifer was six inches taller and several years ahead in school did not enter the equation. Living so deeply within books and imagined stories, I saw everyone around me as characters in the drama; looking out from an inner eye, I was unable to see how I stacked up against the others. Sometimes I felt I was the mother. Jennifer encouraged this. Early on, perhaps even before I was born, she had abdicated her rights—first as eldest, then as daughter. This left her free to wear jeans, to climb trees, to race her younger brother and win. Her body was narrow and gracefully strong, a boy's body.

The scepter passed to me, who, like my mother, seemed suited, in body and temperament, to domesticity. To this day, people meeting Jennifer and me for the first time, together, assume I am the older sister. It's not our bodies; mine was forced early on into a diet and exercise regimen that has counteracted the genetic plumpness that skipped Jennifer and settled in me. And it's not our faces; we are equally lined and faded. It's something else, per-haps the way I hover, fluffing lint from her sweater, the way I reach for the car keys first, find my way to the driver's seat. And the way she allows it.

THE DIFFERENCES in our teenage years, our comings of age, were the differences between the Everly Brothers and the Stones, between the Sandpipers and the Beatles, Paul Anka and Janis Joplin, between garter belts and pantyhose, the diaphragm and the pill. In 1965, good girls did not do it; if they did, they got married. In 1969, everyone did it. Most of my friends announced this to their parents, then proceeded to the pharmacy for a three-month supply of the pill. The rest of us, those with parents who did not seem to understand that it was 1969, developed "menstrual irregularities" that required "medication." Our doctors acquiesced; our mothers kept our secret; our fathers never knew.

In the space between those years, Jennifer got married. She and my mother sewed bridesmaid dresses from bolts of dotted swiss in graduated shades of sherbet—lime, lemon, raspberry, blueberry. Since childhood, Jennifer had had an artist's eye for color and design. Laid out on the bed, the dresses were a watercolor palette, not unlike the one she dabbed at on Saturday mornings while I baked or cleaned beside my mother. Later, before the altar, the four dresses formed a rainbow encircling a cloud—a bride in a hand-stitched dress with a bodice so slim that, thirty years later, my adolescent nieces cannot squeeze into it.

WHEN did her boy's body, narrow and strong, stop being enough? She complained that her trousseau peignoirs hung too straight, that she could not fill the bottoms of her lounging pajamas.

IN THE SPACE after my sister lost her virginity and before I lost mine—how strange, after all these decades, that we still name it a *loss*—I visited her on Saturdays. She and her husband lived in a two bedroom apartment in an old building. The apartment had wooden floors and high ceilings, features that were not fashionable in 1967, when brides and grooms were signing leases on shag-carpeted, air conditioned garden apartments in "complexes" with swimming pools and rec rooms. One bedroom was given over to Jennifer's art projects—sewing, painting, stenciling, woodworking—which she pursued evenings, between the time she came home from her job at a typesetting firm and the time her husband returned late from work or school or wherever he went.

The other bedroom was simply that: a room with a bed, usually unmade. There was a sweet, heavy scent in the air. Gowns and pajamas were draped across bedposts and on closet door-knobs. Beneath the bed, on her husband's side, was a cache of *Penthouse* magazines and paperback novels by Harold Robbins. On the nightstand on her side of the bed was a box of tissues, a jar of Vaseline, and an alarm clock, its round face turned to the wall. Inside her nightstand drawer—of course I looked—was a book called *The Power of Sexual Surrender.* I wondered how much of it had sunk in. When she was fifteen and I was eleven, one day I came home from a girlfriend's house in joyous terror, having just devoured four chapters of a sex manual we'd stolen from her parents' bedroom. Jennifer was sitting at my mother's Singer, serging buttonholes for a pink gingham blouse she would wear on a date that weekend. She had dates every weekend. A string of boys—all of whom resembled Ken dolls—escorted her to movies and sock hops and the bowling alley.

I immediately confronted Jennifer with the discovery, demanding to know why she'd been keeping it all from me. We often shared a room and had few, if any, secrets.

"Keeping what?" she said, her brown eyes blinking.

"Sex, of course," I said. "What else?" And I began describing, in full-color detail, what I'd just learned. As I spoke, her eyes grew wider. Her hands, resting on the pink gingham bunched beneath the buttonholer, did not move. When I was finished, she sighed deeply, stared a moment straight ahead, then went back to her sewing. I knew in that moment that it was all news to her, and I had not broken it well.

AFTER her marriage, she began to look tired, older, a housewife's face on a tomboy's body. When she came to the door on Saturday mornings, she was in her robe. She stayed in it all day. I'd fix lunches, which she would refuse, preferring to nibble at the saltines she carried in the pocket of her robe. All day she floated, unmoored, from the couch to the chair to the couch to the stereo, where the same albums kept replaying themselves—Frankie Avalon, Bobby Vinton, Rod McKuen's *Listen to the Warm*.

SORTING through attic papers, I find these words from Roethke's "To My Sister" copied in my hand, the paper folded, refolded, the creases smudged with age:

> Recall the gradual dark the snow's unmeasured fall
> The naked fields the cloud's immaculate folds
>
> . . . .
>
> Walk boldly my sister but do not deign to give
> Remain secure from pain preserve thy hate thy heart

When did I first sense her gradual dark? There is no date on the paper.

DECADES LATER she told me she'd slept for years. "I remember the pattern on the couch," she said. "Mauve roses." She said for hours at a time she could not lift her head. Only the plump, polished bodies of her sons, thirteen months apart, gave her pleasure. But as the months dragged on, whole days alone with them, whole nights, their bodies became a Bosch nightmare, all mouth and diaper—sucking, slurping, screaming, shitting. Although Jennifer did not say *shitting*.

She told me she couldn't remember, for the life of her, how she got through the days, how the boys got fed, bathed, clothed.

"I wish I'd known," I said. "I would have helped. I had no idea—they always looked so clean. And those sweet, matching outfits."

"I know," she said. "I've seen the pictures. But I can't remember sewing those clothes. I remember the sound of the Singer—maybe I thought someone else was sitting at it. I don't know what I thought."

THERE HAS ALWAYS BEEN, deep inside Jennifer, a place where she could go. My mother is that way. But the landscapes within them are different, or so I imagine. Mother's is liquid, blue, religious; she enters it as she enters water, wholly, receptive, her eyes closing softly. Jennifer's entry is harder, a headfirst push against rock, a trembling; the rock splits, she enters. The space inside the rock closes around her. It is not soft, but it is safe and quiet and dark, and she can sleep.

PREGNANCY temporarily granted the body her marriage demanded—generous breasts, plumped derriere, the comfort of thighs. This is the Jennifer I remember, standing at the stove in our mother's kitchen, stirring. As I look back over the space of thirty years, it seems her whole life was present in that gesture. Safe, for a moment, in her father's house, stirring with her mother's spoon.

She fled back to that space once: lifted her head from the couch, packed matching suitcases for her sons, strapped them into the back seat and drove two thousand miles to my parents' home. "There was nothing else to do," she recalls. "One more day and I would have died." She told her husband it did not have to be permanent, but it had to be *now.* She got a job as a window dresser at Sears. Every day she'd wrestle manikins to the display room floor, force their stiff legs into trousers and shirts, their toeless feet into loafers. "Their eyes don't blink," she said. "They're painted on. They just stare up at you."

SHE's the only person on the planet who calls me *kid.* She's been doing it for several years now, a habit acquired from her second husband. Once a week, at least, she phones, and we talk across three time zones. "How ya doing, kid?" she says. She has no idea how glad this makes me. I'm tired of being the eldest, weary of the space where it forces me to be. Over the past few years, even my parents have started looking up to me. "We appreciate everything you do," they say. "The way you take care of everyone."

"I don't," I tell them. "I really don't."

So when Jennifer calls, I'm happy, the way a kid is happy, expecting nothing, remembering less. I stretch the phone cord as far as it will go, lie flat on the carpet, close my eyes, and listen to her voice the way I used to when we lay in twin beds beside each other. She's a cosmetologist now. It almost pays the bills; her master's degree didn't. She knows the names of the bones in the head, the chemistry of mixing colors. She knows why so many older women have blue hair, and how to avoid it. "It's a science," she says, "but also an art, if you do it right." She can tweeze brows, dye them for a natural look, perform hair removal in the bikini area of women or drag queens. She still has the Styrofoam head she bought in beauty school, the one she practiced on. She named it Marie Antoinette. None of the other students got the joke, and she didn't try to explain it. "They're all so young," she tells me. "They could be my daughters. Sometimes I feel so old."

"You're not," I say. "You look like a teenager."

"You're prejudiced," she says. Then she's on to her son's up-coming wedding, the dress she will wear, how glad she is that he found such a wonderful girl. "*Woman,* I mean," she says. "We call them women now."

WHAT I SAID about Jennifer and books, the part about her living outside the words, is not quite accurate. There was that one night. I woke to the sound of crying. Jennifer's bed had not been slept in, and across the room she was bent over her desk. The book was *The Brothers Karamazov.* She was in tenth grade and there was a test the next day. But she wasn't crying about the test, I could tell by the quality of the weeping. I never learned which lines in the book, which words, had entered her so completely. For me it would be "My brother used to ask the birds to forgive him."

"What's wrong?" I asked.

She shook her head and did not answer. A dim reading light illuminated her face, hollowing out cheekbones I hadn't known were there. A cloudlike quiet moved through the room, the kind that cannot be consoled, a gradual darkening that takes years to lift.

dependent

IN ONE of my earliest memories, my mother is standing on an unpacked crate beneath the ceiling of a Quonset hut. Barefoot, she balances like a circus performer, testing her weight gingerly as she leans toward the curved wall, trying to hang a picture of waves. This is the only image in my head that hints at any desperation my mother might have felt in her long career as a military wife. If hers was a war against rootlessness and loneliness, she fought it privately, in small physical skirmishes. She made a home from whatever was given. If the kitchen in our new quarters had a window, she'd size it up as we walked through the empty rooms. The next morning, I'd wake to find she'd stitched and hung yellow curtains, creating an illusion of sunlight that tinted the linoleum and bounced off the toaster she'd polished with her sleeve.

My father was like her in this way; he did what he could to shield us from the difficulties of military life. Since he was a marine, we could not accompany him on overseas assignments, some of which lasted fifteen months. And since he was an officer, we were able to stay in one place longer than the families of enlisted men. Except for a few months in temporary quarters—the

Quonset hut, an apartment building, the officers' guest suite—we lived in sturdy houses within driving distance of the base. As we approached the gate, the uniformed guard would glance at the sticker on the windshield of our station wagon, click his heels together, and salute. We children would salute back. If our father was present, he'd reprimand us, reminding us that a military salute was not to be taken lightly.

Once out of our father's sight, we took it lightly, as we took lightly everything related to the military. Cushioned from hardships, we saw the base as one privilege after another—free swimming, dime movies, twenty-five-cent bowling and miniature golf, discount toys at the PX, cheap groceries (unlike our neighbors with their civilian pints of ice cream, we never had less than a gallon in our freezer). The only privilege we did not welcome was free medical care, which seemed to encourage our mother to splurge on tetanus shots and throat cultures.

I was vaguely aware that our sense of privilege stemmed from the fact that our father was an officer, and occasionally I caught glimpses of what my life would have been like had my father been, say, a corporal instead of a major—and later, a lieutenant colonel. On our way to the base swimming pool, I counted the stucco duplexes surrounded by dirt yards where khakis and diapers flapped on makeshift lines. Children's faces were plugged to the front window, hostages along with their carless mothers, while we whipped by in our blue station wagon, creating dust swirls that must have settled minutes later on their wet laundry.

Turn another page in the story, take the next bend in the road, and it was time to leave again—the luggage carrier packed to the gills, the U-Haul trailing. Yet no matter how many times we moved, how many friends and towns we left behind, there was always a passel of warm bodies to fill the station wagon and the empty new house. We were our own portable town; my siblings were my constant allies. Of course we fought (the veins in my brother's forehead pulsing as he lunged toward me), but when the dust settled and the blood cooled, peace was always restored. The more heated the battle, the more dramatic the truce that followed. We knew better than to turn on each other permanently, for soon we'd be moving to a new town where strangers waited at the bottom of the U-Haul ramp. In the long run, we were all we had. Because we had each other, we never felt alone.

And never homeless, for in the distance was our grandparents' farm where we returned every summer. To the same featherbeds, the haymow with the rotting floorboards, the attic crammed with outgrown clothing, the worn path to the creek. We were hybrids—half marine, half farmer—and whenever we grew tired of packing and unpacking, we knew the farm would be there. Old as dirt, the saying goes. The land would be waiting for us. I was born a marine brat and spent my childhood in service, but until my twenty-first year, my life had been lined with escape hatches. Except for one brief remembrance—Mother hanging a picture of waves—nothing prepared me for my stint as a military wife.

I'D BEEN MARRIED less than a year, and everything that could have gone wrong, had. Pete's parents had divorced, and his father had been hospitalized with severe bleeding ulcers. When Pete quit two consecutive jobs because he refused to take orders from supervisors, I doubled up on my hours at the printing shop and continued full-time studies at the university. A brilliant linguist, Pete had been studying for a degree in German, but at the height of the Vietnam war, his student deferment was cancelled. A few weeks later he received his draft lottery number. It was a low number, which almost guaranteed that he would be drafted. And almost all draftees were sent to the front lines. If he joined the army, rather than wait to be drafted, he might avoid an infantry assignment. Then again, he might not.

I tried to comfort him, but with each step I took toward him, he took two steps away. Being a wife, I'd come to believe, was not something I was good at. Pete's fingernails were chewed to the quick, and the tic on the side of his face had intensified, the spasms more frequent than ever. The draft was breathing outside our door, and we were holed up behind it. I felt helpless, under siege from without and within.

Then, just as the draft was about to break down the door, Pete uncovered a window. Following a tip from a fellow German student, he took a qualifying exam and won a coveted slot at the army's language institute, four hundred miles up the California coast. The timing, it seemed, could not have been better. It would take Pete two months to finish basic training and three more months to complete the introductory language course. Then he'd send for me. In the meantime, if I moved in with my parents, I could quit my job at the print shop and finish my literature degree. I told myself that this turn of events would also be good for Pete: He could escape Vietnam while being paid to study languages.

My father had never been fond of Pete, but as soon as Pete joined the army, my father's feelings seemed to soften, and for one brief moment I imagined my husband and father joining forces, their arms linked, rocking me between them as in a child's game. The day Pete left for boot camp, I stored our belongings and moved back to my parents' home—my father had recently retired from the marines. Jennifer and Tom had left for marriage and college long before, and Claudia and Rick, having claimed the empty bedrooms for their own, were not about to relinquish their privacy. I moved in with my youngest sister, Lana, who had recently turned nine. Several times over the first few weeks, I looked up from the book I was studying to see a little girl standing beside Lana in the doorway, staring at me silently. Each time it was a different little girl. Later I learned that Lana was charging her friends a quarter to see the bride who was now her roommate. She'd told them that my husband had been killed in the war, and did they want to see the veil?

Every night as I climbed into our shared double bed, I felt a great relief. Surrounded by Lana's stuffed animals and the nursery rhyme comforter, I was rocked backward into another time. I slept longer and deeper than I'd slept since I'd left my parents' home. And waking to the clatter and bang of breakfast, my mother working in the kitchen, was a pleasure so exquisite I couldn't imagine why I'd ever left. These feelings worried me. I had a husband. Shouldn't I be missing him?

I wondered if my mother had ever felt this way. When my father was overseas, she stayed busy every daylight hour; I never saw her cry. But on nights when insomnia claimed her, I'd wake to the sounds of table legs scraping across the wooden floor, casters squeaking as the sofa was rolled to one spot then another, the electric mixer whirring, the rat-a-tat-tat of the Singer accelerating to unsafe speeds. Then the pause. The quiet. The click of the presser-foot being lifted, and in the space between seams, fragments of a top-ten song from the radio. I'd lie in the dark, wondering if they were playing American songs where my father was—in Japan or Korea or Hawaii or Vietnam. For years I counted the distances between my parents in time zones I traced in the *Rand McNally Atlas.* Their lives, it seemed, ran smoothly on separate, parallel tracks. The moment my father returned, the tracks converged, the double seam healed, and only the white strip on his arm, the place where his Japanese watch had lain, recorded the lost time.

Reunited, their bodies made a spoon curve on the sofa—my mother in a pink housedress with covered snaps, my father behind her with his hand cupped over her waist. I thought all married people acted that way. It did not occur to me until many years later that their union was not typical, that it lacked the quality of dailiness that dulls the shine on marriages where partners eat and work together and sleep beside each other every night. The Marine Corps built a wall of time and distance, a wall my parents were forced to scale again and again to reach each other. Perhaps that's why their marriage wore so well, and why they had so many children. My aunt tells of the day, forty-five years ago, when my mother announced she was pregnant again. The child would be her fifth. The fourth, Claudia, was nursing at my mother's breast. My aunt's reaction to the news was, "How could you let it happen again?" My mother simply shrugged her shoulders and laughed: "I'm just always so happy to see him."

WEEKS grew to months. I began to miss the sputter of Pete's motorcycle in the driveway, the damp fossil his feet left on the bathroom rug. I missed his blue eyes, his rough freckled hands and his smell, an odd mixture of motorcycle oil, cigarettes, and English Leather. Surprised by the force of my longing, I wondered if Pete was missing me too. Maybe the army was what we'd needed all along.

The day Pete called to say our apartment was ready, I rented a

U-Haul van. My father and Rick loaded the furniture; in the cab I piled clothes, boxes of books, my grandmother's Wedding Ring quilt, my framed diploma in English literature, and my mother's portable Singer. Early the next morning I was on my way, driving the first leg of the four-hundred-mile journey up the California coastline. How many times through how many years had my mother made a journey like this while my father waited for her in their new quarters hundreds of miles away? On the radio Roberta Flack was singing "The First Time Ever I Saw Your Face." Sun glinted off the waves. With each tick of the odometer, the difficulties of the past year receded like the images in my rearview mirror. Suspended on the road between my parents and my husband, with the ocean to my left and the sun overhead, I felt hopeful. A fresh start in a new place. Things were going to be better.

But the man who met me at the base welcome station was not the man I had married. His eyes were gray, not blue. He was thinner. He had poked an extra hole in his belt to cinch the trousers around his waist, and the fabric puckered above his buttocks and thighs. When I ran to hug him, my legs weak from the ten-hour drive, his kiss was hurried and dry. He smelled of beer and an unfamiliar brand of cigarettes. The tic was alive on his cheek. When we got to our quarters, we made love on a pallet spread on the living-room floor, but the lovemaking was as hurried as his kiss had been, and as dry.

MILITARY dependents is what they were called, the wives and children living beside us, below us, and on top of us, in apartments identical to our own. Theirs was another world, one I'd never seen from the inside, the underground world of the enlisted. The officers' wives I'd known throughout childhood had been anything but dependent. With their husbands gone for months, sometimes years at a time, these women not only shopped, cooked, cleaned, and sewed, but balanced checkbooks, mowed lawns, made house and car repairs, and negotiated all necessary public business. If their responsibilities were doubled, so were their freedoms. They came and went as they pleased, subservient only to their own needs and the needs of their children. When my father was overseas, our household ran on a different clock. We stayed up later, slept later, played more games, ate more child-friendly foods—beanie weenies, macaroni and cheese, fish sticks, Frito loaf, and my favorite, a dish I named Train Wreck, a Sunday night treat in which the week's leftovers collided in one large iron skillet, topped with Tabasco sauce and sopped up with white Wonder bread.

And over it all, my mother presided. I never doubted her authority or her ability to keep us safe and happy. She moved easily through the days and nights with a grace I associated with *her* mother. Poor farmers are another breed of independent women. Partnered by necessity, they work as equals beside their husbands in field, garden, and pasture. Both my grandmothers, trained in self-sufficiency, not only managed the indoor chores expected of farm wives (stoking kitchen fires, frying chickens, making sausage) but also chopped the wood that made those fires possible, wielded saw and hammer to build chicken coops, repaired the fences that encircled the hogs waiting to be slaughtered. This was my heritage, a legacy of independence passed from grandmother to mother to daughter.

But there were no pastures on this army base, no squads of officers' wives gathering at the pool or golf course. The young military wives who surrounded me were trapped without cars, without jobs, with two or three preschool children crammed into a two-bedroom apartment, their only escape Wednesday night bingo or a rerun at the base theater. Or morning classes in the damp windowless basement they called the Craft House, where they painted ceramic Santas, Virgin Marys, pumpkins, and elves while their children scuffled on a rug at the child care center, overseen by women with bad teeth who stared at the television bolted high to the wall.

Despite what my ID card proclaimed, my laminated face and name stamped with the word "dependent," I was determined never to become one of those quietly nervous women I saw in the laundromat of the apartment complex. I renewed my prescription for birth control pills, hung my diploma over the kitchen sink, and set about camouflaging the apartment. I covered the khaki walls with daisy contact paper, painted a Seven Sisters constellation on the bathroom ceiling, and strung a mobile of kites and balloons over the dinette table. I draped my grandmother's quilt over the couch, and at the windows I hung colored beads that rattled when an occasional civilian breeze found its way through the maze of concrete hallways that led to our third-floor unit.

THE LANGUAGE institute position might have been a plum, an assignment draftees would have killed for, but it was still the army. Privates like my husband still stood inspection, still pulled KP and all-night guard duty, a task made all the more demeaning by the fact that they were issued shovels instead of rifles. It was a pretend war, the enlistees were constantly reminded, but to Pete it might as well have been Vietnam. Each order given, each exam, was an enemy rustling in the bushes. In sleep he thrashed at the covers, and when I reached to calm him, his chest was beaded with sweat.

Late one night I woke in an empty bed. I called Pete's name and searched the apartment, and when I looked out the window I saw him slouched inside a phone booth across the street, his boots pressed against the glass. He had left the door open to darken the booth, but the streetlight silhouetted his lean body. One hand held the phone against his cheek; the other hand caressed the cord, his fingers running up and down its uncoiled length. Suddenly what had encased him, the exoskeleton of phone booth and bone, of boots and jacket, fell away, and what had been invisible to me came into microscopic focus. It wriggled on the slide—blood and tissue, muscle, the soft inner membranes—a secret life pulsing on its own. I knew that he was talking to a woman.

I ran a bath and soaked until my fingertips were shriveled. Only four more months, I told myself. Then the Chinese course will be over and we'll leave for the next base, but this time I'll be with him from the first day on. And I'll be pregnant—that way, he can't leave. Until then I'll wait it out. You can survive anything for four months. I climbed out of the tub, powdered and creamed my body, combed the tangles from my hair and sat by the space heater until my hair was silky, spilling over my folded knees like the hair of the Oriental woman in the painting my father brought back from overseas the summer I turned twelve.

An hour later, perhaps two, Pete climbed into bed. When I asked where he'd been, he turned his face to the window. I never asked again, not when he began disappearing for hours at a time, not when he stayed out all night. I put the unpacking on hold and attended to him. I would cook more of his favorite foods, steam his khakis with a cleaner pleat. This thing I was living was my life.

EVEN WHEN I missed the second period, the possibility of pregnancy still didn't occur to me. I'd been sleeping fitfully, troubled by a low-grade nausea that weakened my appetite, and as a result, I'd lost several pounds. Yet my body felt strangely heavier. My breasts had begun to swell, and there was a strange metallic taste in my mouth. One night I woke with a tightness in my belly, a wrenching, as if something were twisting me from the inside, a vise clamping down.

Pete stirred but did not wake as I left the bed. At the bathroom door, I flicked on the light. The fluorescent tube above the sink flickered, went black, buzzed, and flickered again, coloring the room in a bluish wash. The toilet seat was cold. The vise gripped me again. I concentrated on the veins in my thighs, tracing the intricate network, and when the vise came again, I closed my eyes and pushed the pain out my mouth in rapid, nearly silent animal pants.

When I finally stood and looked down, what I saw was the size of a man's outspread hand. I watched it floating, a viscous crimson island, watched the edges peel away into strands that thinned and separated, marbling the water with pink streams, leaving only a thick dark center. Then I lifted off. My bloodied nightgown billowed, and I rose toward the ceiling where my mother and grandmother were waiting. *What took you so long?* read the cartoon bubbles over their heads. Long fingers reached out to me, caressing the sleeves of my gown. We hung there suspended, looking down at the scene below, where a woman's hand was reaching for the chrome handle. I heard the flush and saw the water swirling in ribbons of red and pink and black, a child's pinwheel spinning dizzy circles.

A FEW WEEKS before the scheduled move, my mother arrived to help out. Boxes were stacked in the living room. The walls were bare once again. "Looks like you've got everything under control," she said brightly, but I could tell she had sensed trouble. As the hours passed she kept checking the clock; she never asked where Pete was. "You look thin," was all she said. "Are you eating enough?" She spent the evening at the Singer, altering my dresses and mending Pete's civilian clothes. I lay on the bed, comforted by the whir of the machine, the drumming regularity of the stitches. It was a rhythm as old as my first memory of her, lulling me into a safe place. I sat up on the bed.

"He's having an affair. I know who she is. He's there right now." My mother's lips, pressed together to secure a family of straight pins, opened, and the pins scattered to the floor. I told her everything—about the dark-haired neighbor, about walking in on her and Pete in the laundromat. I told her that the woman's husband was overseas, that I suspected it had been going on even before I'd arrived, and that now every evening when I went outside Pete was on the playground with her sons, pushing them on the swings or throwing baseballs he'd bought at the PX. I said I couldn't wait another minute, that I was going to the woman's apartment to confront him, to ask him to come home.

My mother raised her hand as if hailing an invisible cab. Her index finger was cocked. Then slowly her hand drifted down.

Her eyes brimmed for an instant, cleared. "Do what you need to do," is all she said.

I knew the words she was holding back. *She* would not have gone. Years before I'd overheard her comforting a neighbor. Women often came to my mother for help pinning up a hem or doctoring a fevered child, and one neighbor came by often, her face tight and red, the seams in her stockings a little skewed. On this particular night, she was crying fitfully and loud, the way I thought only children cried, those sobs that lift your shoulders and deepen your voice.

"What. Would. You. Do," the woman cried, each syllable punctuated by a jerky intake of breath.

My mother's voice was even and calm. "I've never had cause to doubt him. I would swear by it."

"But. What. If. He. Did." It's the kind of question you ask when you're desperate. What you want is for the other person to tell you it's okay, to pat your hand and say everything will be all right. My mother gave the truth, and I could tell by her tone that she meant it. I could also tell that she had considered the question more than once and the decision had been reached long before this moment. Her words flowed like water:

"I'd walk out the door and never look back. The more I loved him, the faster I'd walk."

"But. What. About money? Where would you go?"

"I'd live in a shack before I'd take a penny of his money."

"But. The children."

"We'd manage."

I sat on the bed and looked across the room at my mother. Her dark eyes, lit with anger and pain, held no answers. In desperation I reached back in memory, past my mother's eyes, past her fierce pride, searching for another way to finish this, a way that would better suit me.

What I saw was Grandma Sylvie cutting off the dying dog's leg to save him. *Whatever it takes, you do.* Then I saw her decades before I was born, standing at the back door of the farmhouse, with two children at her side and a baby, my mother, asleep in her arms. Suitcases are stacked beside her and she is facing my grandfather. Her words are like bullets. "Look at that woman again, and we're gone."

I don't know how long she stood there before he gave his answer. Knowing my grandmother, not long. My grandfather must have played his part well, for she never took that first step through the door, into the garage and the waiting car. The scene freezes in that moment—the suitcases, my grandmother's silent stare, my mother waking in her arms as if from a bad dream, releasing a strong hoarse cry.

THE MARRIAGE ended at the runway of a California airport where I boarded a plane to Columbia, South Carolina, my brother's city. After I'd confronted Pete with my knowledge of the other woman, we'd attempted a half-hearted reconciliation, but it soon became clear that he was not going to end the affair. "And even if I did," he said one night during dinner, "I can't promise that it won't happen again." I looked across the table at him, and the years stretched out before me. I knew I couldn't live that way. I packed my bags that night.

Once in South Carolina, I underwent the initiation rites common to newly separated women. I wept, lost weight, cut my hair, found a minimum-wage job, bought a used car, rented a studio apartment. Fort Jackson was a few miles away, and over the next few months I often found myself cruising its perimeter. My half of our furniture was delivered to me courtesy of the United States Army. Officially I was still a dependent and would be for another year, the grace period the army had extended to me. Desperately close to the poverty line—I now qualified for food stamps—I told myself I could use the services. I needed groceries, I was past due for a medical exam, and my first troublesome wisdom tooth was starting to push through.

When the long-distance divorce decree arrived in the mail, I contested nothing. With one signature, I swept away the previous three years, agreeing to no fault on either side. Only one remnant of the marriage remained: my military ID card, which I found, to my surprise, I did not wish to relinquish. It had taken months to mourn the marriage, the man, and the almost-child. But my tour of duty was not over. Something yet remained, a loss that ambushed me one winter afternoon as I was driving past the base. This time, my car turned, headed toward the front gate, and stopped. I pulled the ID card from my wallet and held it out to the guard. With a snappy salute, he motioned me forward. It might have been any of a dozen bases I'd known. Fort Ord, Fort Belvoir, Fort Meade, Quantico, El Toro, Corpus Christi. Bases named for generals, chiefs, bulls, the bodies of lesser and greater gods. Bases so familiar I could have driven their streets in my dreams—and I had, many times since I'd left California. I'd also been dreaming my future, in dreams that took place outside the gates of the military and prefigured the circumstances of my new life—a new husband and a home on a civilian street, a marriage secure though childless, the death of my grandmother and of the farm.

Once inside the gates of Fort Jackson, it felt as natural as breathing, this tour past the barracks, the commissary, the PX, past the swimming pool and tennis courts with their tall fences, the officers' quarters and the Quonset huts. My gums were aching. The tip of the wisdom tooth had pushed through the surface, and my swollen jaw was pulsing with pain. I passed the clinic once, twice, then circled back to the parking lot. I stopped my car and sat for a few minutes, staring at the entrance and watching the parade of soldiers and dependents. A woman emerged holding the hand of a little girl who was rubbing her upper arm (a vaccination, I suspected) and sporting an imitation medal on her shirt, some army doctor's award for courage in battle. I'd earned the right, I told myself. Even the army thought so—that's why they called it a grace period. I got out of the car and walked toward the clinic, tonguing the swollen gum. No question about it, the tooth would have to go.

earth, air, fire, and father

MY FATHER won the Distinguished Flying Cross for "a series of daring attacks on his objective" whereby he succeeded in destroying one fuel vehicle and two supply-laden trucks. These attacks occurred on April 25, 1952, about the time I was lisping my first complete sentences, none of which contained the word *father*. Forty-two years later, when I arrived for a visit to my parents' midwestern home, my father was leafing through a scrapbook into which he had gathered the memorabilia of nearly thirty years of military service. A shadow box of medals, newly framed behind glass, hung on the wall above his head. When I asked to see the scrapbook, he eagerly obliged. And as he turned each page, slowly, reverently, for an instant time stood on its head. I was the parent, he the eager child, spreading his prizes before me.

My father, to my knowledge, had never needed the approval of any of his six children. Certainly he never asked for it. The Paul McClanahan of my childhood was clear-eyed, sure-footed, each forward step of his life deliberate and purposeful, or so it had seemed to me. Yet in this small gesture—turning the pages, looking up as if expecting a nod—the pattern of his life seemed to split apart. Had my father foreseen the breaking? Was this the reason for the scrapbook, for the framed box that housed the pieces of his past? Here was order, an arrangement both logical and aesthetic—and, for the first time, open for display. My father's life as Aviator Number P18825 had always been hidden from my view. "He's flying missions" was my answer when friends asked about his long absences. *Missions* was my mother's word. It had a holy sound to it, the vague ring of sacrifice and honor.

MY MOTHER often emerges from the depths of memory, her legs scissoring the water. Never my father. In the officers' pool at one base or another, we children would bob, held aloft in my mother's wake, while my father stood on the concrete, his feet so smooth and dry they might have been buffed. Tributaries of blue vein branched from his toes and disappeared into trousers cuffed twice, in case of splashes. I unrolled the mystery of my father inch by inch, by begging stories from my mother and imagining the rest. Since I possessed few facts, the possibilities for invention were all the more radiant. The details varied from telling to telling, but two elements remained constant. My father was a pilot. His territory was the sky. When I dreamed of him, the dreams were weightless, colorless, suffused with ether. Only when his returning plane touched down on the tarmac did the weight of the world register, and for the next few months my dreams took on the bulk and permanence of earth, grounded in part by the gifts he brought back: hibachi pots, yo-yos, transistor radios, bolts of raw silk. Once he filled the bathtub with lobsters; none of us children had ever seen one. I remember the clicking of claws against porcelain, but I can't remember eating the lobsters. Seafood was not part of my childhood food history, and it certainly hadn't been a part of my father's.

As a child of tenant farmers in Illinois, the nearest thing to a river my father knew was the horse trough flowing between two barns. Often the well was dry. Every Saturday night his mother boiled kettles of rainwater and emptied them into a metal tub that had been dragged to the middle of the kitchen floor, beside the wood stove. The youngest children were bathed first. The babies, my aunt remembers, would sometimes pee in the water. My father was a middle child, so I imagine that when his turn finally came, the water was slick with soap shavings and scum. I see him sitting in the tub, his blond head bowed over knees folded for modesty's sake. His mother pours another kettle of warm water. Steam rises around him like a cloud. Not long before, his mother had robbed herself of butter money so that she could take Paul for a barnstormer's sightseeing trip over their little town. Since then he has been daydreaming of lifting over plow and silo, tearing a hole through the sky.

Sometimes the dream comes while Paul is in the field, but he pushes it down. To lose concentration, even for an instant, could cost him an eye—such is the speed and propulsion of the ears of corn that fly from his father's hands. In the furrow of the Great Depression, tenant shuckers got three cents a bushel, and with the help of his son, Grandpa Clarence could harvest a hundred bushels a day, one and a half acres of another man's fields. Clarence worked from first light to dusk, and Paul joined him in the field when he got home from school. In my mind, it is evening, not yet lantern light. A slender boy—hair the color of corn tassels—is working the down row. He bends his back and dodges the ears flying toward the wagon. His right hand is strapped in a shucking hook, the metal thumb protruding like a weapon as the ears, in one swift motion, are grabbed, ripped open, and tossed toward the backboard of the horse-drawn wagon. Clarence has trained Paul to keep a straight eye, to fix his attention on the stalk before him. They must shuck two more rows before dark.

ONE SPRING Clarence's plow mare gave birth to a colt my father raised, then sold to finance his senior year in high school and a trip to Cincinnati, where he signed up for a four year stint in the United States Marine Corps. The yellowed document pasted in the scrapbook records the moment: "Said Paul Glenn McClanahan was born 7 February 1922 at Arcola, Illinois; when enlisted was 68 inches high with blue eyes, brown hair, ruddy complexion." It feels strange to see my father characterized in inches, as if he were some wind-up toy soldier one might order from a catalog.

His memories of basic training are sparse, the result of years of conscious forgetting. What he remembers, against his will, is being shouted out of bed at four A.M. to stand in the dark with dozens of other recruits who chanted in unison until they were hoarse: "I am nothing. I am a piece of dirt. I sleep with my rifle. I love my rifle. I am nothing without my gun."

After basic training my father was promoted to private first class, corporal, and sergeant, but his flight dreams were yet to be realized. He spent two years as a gunner on the battleship *Texas*, patrolling the North Atlantic with convoys, and though he was a good marksman, he took little pleasure in the act. In this way, and in others, he was unlike his father, one of those men for whom sighting down a barrel is a focusing event, a moment in which the undiffused elements of one's life narrow to one perfect point.

My father never got his sea legs, but after a few days he was able to conquer the pitch and roll of the neatly holystoned deck. Woozy and homesick, he sent letters to his mother and cartons of Camels to his father. In a hammock strung between overhead hooks, he tried to sleep. Days he chipped paint from the deck, studied for his commission, cleaned weapons, typed reports, polished shoes and badges; nights he stood watch from a crow's nest, taking aim at anything that moved. Finally in 1943 he tried out his first wings in the Marine Corps Glider Pilot School, where he was trained to chase clouds, searching thermal updrafts. Sometimes, to gain altitude, the instructor would dive the J3 Cub directly into thunderheads where winds reached one hundred miles per hour. But the sailplane proved too light a burden for the approaching world of war. Just days before he married my mother, my father was promoted from naval cadet to second lieutenant and completed the naval aviation training for heavier-than-air aircraft.

Only one obstacle remained, the final hurdle my father feared would mean the end of his dream. At an Olympic-sized pool in Athens, Georgia, where the young aviators-to-be had been assembled for the AAA Swimming Test, the officials strapped his buddy Tom to my father's back, ordering my father to swim him to safety. "Play dead!" the sergeant called, and Tom fell limp. Halfway across the pool, my father went under. He gulped and surfaced, sank beneath the double weight, surfaced again. "Swim!" my father gurgled to his buddy. "Paddle, or I'm dead!" My father never forgot the favor; he named his first son Tom.

ONE AUTUMN day while our family was stationed at Quantico Air Base, we drove to Arlington National Cemetery, my father steering through acre after acre of smoothly mown hills that seemed to ripple and surge around us, lapping at the sides of the blue station wagon. I was ten years old, and from where I sat, my face pressed to the window, the white crosses resembled the masts of sailboats—thousands upon thousands of identical boats sailing in perfectly spaced formations. At the end of our voyage we docked at the parking lot and my father led us, in silence, up a sloping terrace to a large marble monument set atop a slab of concrete. I whispered to my sister that this soldier must have been very important, to get the biggest grave. My father hushed me with his eyes. For the next several minutes we stood at attention, stiff-legged and silent, watching a guard in full military dress pace before the monument. His right hand, gloved in white, supported a rifle from the tip of which a bayonet sprouted.

There was no name on the grave. The inscription read only "An American Soldier," followed by words to the effect that this soldier was known only to God. Apparently that was the whole point. The fact that no one knew who was buried in the tomb made the soldier's sacrifice even more supreme. And there were lots more like him, the plaque said—hundreds of dead soldiers whose names we will never know. I nudged my younger sister Claudia and pointed to the date on the stone: November 11, Veterans' Day. "Mom's birthday," I whispered smugly, storing the rest for the drive home. I had recently learned the story behind my mother's middle name, Armista, and for months I had been boasting to friends—the way a child boasts of anything she believes makes her special—that my mother's name meant peace. I was too young to appreciate the irony of a career marine married to Peace. I was simply enjoying the power of my newly found discovery, a power that would cease on the day my brother, wielding a dictionary, set the record straight. "See," Tom said. "It doesn't mean peace at all. It's just a temporary truce. There's a big difference."

LAST YEAR my father made a decision that surprised us all: to be buried at Arlington. Looking back on his life, I suppose that his decision shouldn't have come as a surprise, yet I'd always assumed he'd be buried close to his midwestern roots and the roots of my mother's family. As the spouse of a distinguished marine, she also qualifies for Arlington, but to be buried among strangers is not her first choice. Her parents are buried in Indiana, her baby girl in an Illinois plot that belonged to my father's father, one of the few parcels of land my grandfather ever owned. When Grandpa Clarence died, my parents boarded separate planes—a habit they often followed to ensure that, in the event of a crash, their six children would not be orphaned—and flew to Illinois.

As Clarence's children gathered at the home place, they began to talk, each recounting some incident that set heads to nodding. I wasn't there, of course, but I imagine it went something like this: Oh yes, they remembered the little dispenser Clarence had kept by the kitchen table, the delight of being asked to "roll one" for their father. The taste of glue at the edges of the paper, the bittersweet smell of the loose tobacco, the burning sensation in their nostrils when the match was struck and Clarence put the cigarette to his mouth. Yes, they remembered the tubs of lard after the butchering, the cracklings their mother packed in their lunch tins for special treats, but no, the sisters couldn't recall the fire pit. "That must have been your job, Bud," they said, using my father's nickname.

I imagine my father nodding, and then, after much coaxing, telling of winter mornings when he would follow Clarence past the barn to a clearing where a huge butchering table stood. Together, father and son shoveled from the black soil a pit the size of a grave. After the pit was dug, they gathered kindling and wood, laid a fire, and placed a large steel pot filled with lime and water in the center of the hole. While Clarence cornered the hogs, Paul fired up the pit, coaxing the flames high and blinking against the cinders that flew toward his face. He handed his father the twenty-two and watched as Clarence sighted down the barrel, aiming for the space between the hog's eyes.

Clarence was a good shot—one crack and the hog buckled. "Bud, we saved the squeal on that one," he would say. Then the next hog, and the next. By now the flames were leaping, the water bubbling. They dumped the hogs into the pot, stirred in lime with a long pole, and waited. Sometimes the fates cooperated, hair floating effortlessly to the surface. When the lime didn't do the trick, my grandfather heaved the carcass onto the table and scraped until the hog was smooth. This turned my father's stomach, causing the bile to back up in his throat, but he knew that without this step, there would be no bacon, no ham, no lard rendered in tubs, no intestines for sausage casings, no thick shoulder cured with brown sugar and salt, then wrapped carefully in linen to last all winter. With a butcher's knife Clarence cut the tendon behind the leg and hooked the hog to a singletree. The severed head thudded into a bucket readied for this purpose. One long slice opened up the belly, and bare hands scooped out the entrails. Heat from the innards mixed with the cold air and steamed, clouding the space between them.

"WHAT HAPPENED over there?" I asked again. My father had been evading my questions, and the Flying Cross citation in my hand held no answer. It said only that my father's mission was accomplished "despite hostile antiaircraft fire, mountainous terrain, and low visibility," a vague description that could as easily characterize the obstacles of my father's life.

"It was a night fighter," he began hesitantly. "The F4U Corsair. We flew in complete darkness, except for flares the on-station flare planes set off for us." He always uses "we" when he speaks of his missions, though he flew most of them alone.

I asked if he was ever lonely or scared, flying in the dark. He nodded. "Especially over water. Except for the instrument panel, everything was black for miles around. For hours and hours. Black as far as we could see. But in moonlight, when we flew over snow, it was bright as day."

After a few minutes I saw that he didn't want to talk about the night raids. He wanted to talk about the snow, the unearthly brightness from the heavens, the reflection of the moon. But I couldn't let it go.

"What did you do up there?" I asked again, ignorant as all children should remain.

He looked down at his hands. "I guess Tom was right," he said softly, and immediately I knew which incident he was remembering. At the height of the Vietnam war—or the depths of the war, depending on your perspective—when the last thing a conscientious objector wanted to admit was that his father had flown bombing raids, one night my brother screamed to my father's face, "You're nothing but a hired killer."

"Never mind," I said. "It's not important."

My father closed the scrapbook and shifted his gaze to the window. "They were terrible things we did. It was our job. If it moved, we shot it. Supply trucks, mostly, but we strafed at anything. The napalm was the worst. You could see fire for four or five city blocks, and you knew you had to be hitting more than the target. The world just lit up."

He paused. I waited, certain that he was about to segue into the story I'd heard as a child, the one in which he emerges as a hero: Once, flying over enemy territory, both wings loaded with ammo, the left side of his plane caught fire. He unlatched the cockpit, reached for his parachute, stood up to jump, felt the wind, thought in an instant "None of my friends down *there,*" and decided he'd rather go down *with* the plane than without it. "Anything I can do for you?" radioed the flare plane pilot. "Say thirteen hails," my father answered. "I'm going home."

The silence lengthened. When it broke, my father's voice was a whisper, entering the story *in medias res,* in the middle of snow and darkness in a Korean field. But it was not the hero story. This time he was in the night fighter, loaded with bombs and ammo. He'd strapped himself in, checked his controls, and had just begun his run for takeoff when he felt the impact, felt himself being thrust forward, hard, quick—then the unreal sensation of dangling. He'd hit an embankment, turning the night fighter onto its nose and plunging it deep into snow. He was trapped upside down, the snow icy hot on his neck and back, packing him in. Hours went by, or maybe only minutes. He was shivering, then numb, then sleepy, unable to breathe except in brief, sharp gasps that stung his lungs. Death was coming, he was sure of that. He would either freeze to death or go up in flames; it was just a matter of hours, or minutes. He could see the radio button but could not reach it. He could feel the pistol strapped to his chest. "If I could have reached it," he says, "I would have shot myself." But his arms were packed hard into the snow, frozen above his head in a gesture of surrender. Radio voices floated in and out, calling his name.

LAST NIGHT my father stood calmly in the shallows of my dream and sent one golf ball, then another and another, into the ocean. The club glinted silver beneath a trio of moons, and his eyes were clear bowls where blue fishes darted. All day I've been worrying the dream. Why the senseless waste of golf balls, the nearness of the sea? Dreams of water are dreams of rest, the tranquil letting go of ego and control, the loss of the body itself.

When my father retired, he received an honorable discharge. This celebratory term, which is meant to suggest the release of burden, the final fulfillment of duty, is shadowed by darker meanings. Discharge: to fire, as a weapon; to pour forth the contents; to eliminate energy from a charged body; to unload or empty. One morning, my father's casket will be lifted from its waiting place in the receiving vault at Arlington, beside dozens of others scheduled for burial that day. A horse-drawn caisson, the vehicle once used to transport heavy artillery into battle, will carry my father's body, which, like the bodies of thousands of other soldiers, once served as ammunition for a government's wars. At the grave site a color guard will salute. A bugler will play taps. And as the firing party discharges its duty, emptying three rounds into the air, my father will be released from the body that contained him, the cylinder into which he was dropped. Only a shell will remain, the spent casing of memory.

When I look back on the moments of my life that enclose him, there are few in which all his selves—farm boy, seasick sailor, pilot, bomber, father—show their faces. One is the moment in the den when he closed the scrapbook against my questions. The other goes back a long time. I was eleven or twelve, and my father had just returned from a mission, bringing with him a Japanese hi-fi. It was blond veneer, polished to a blinding sheen, and he set it up in the basement, which had been converted into a bedroom for my brothers. One night I woke to a rotting stench and the clamor of metal buckets. I rushed from bed to join my sisters and brothers, who had taken up their graduated stations on the basement steps. Mother handed us cloths to cover our mouths and noses, explaining that somehow the city sewer had backed up into our house. My brothers could barely contain their excitement—wow, a real flood, look how high it is! Already the bottom bunk was covered, water rising toward the top of the dresser. My father was shirtless, waist deep in filth. His eyes surveyed the damage. Then he lifted the hi-fi above his head and waded toward my mother, shouting, "Get back, Juanita. Take the children upstairs! There could be anything in this water!"

hatching

Seventy years later and she still smells it in her dreams. Ruth is my father's oldest sister, and she tells me this over lunch at an uptown department store in her midwestern city where I have come to visit, hungry for something I am afraid will get lost. Last month she had a triple-bypass. Under the designer pantsuit, she is stitched from breastbone to navel and, again, from groin to ankle where they stripped the vein that would feed her heart. It's not the family tree I seek, not the official line a genealogist is paid to trace. What I need are the small moments, the details, the stories aborted that never found their climax, their denouement. Ragtags of faded dresses, like pieces my grandmothers salvaged and stitched into quilts. Maybe if I listen hard enough, the scraps will come together. And if the quilt is not beautiful, at least it will be warm, something to throw around my shoulders late at night.

The smell in Ruth's dreams is the smell of warm eggs from an incubator that was kept in the bedroom she shared with four sisters. The eggs were in a covered tray with a light bulb hung above for warmth. They were turned once a day. Over the next weeks, one by one the chicks hatched. Usually the girls were asleep when this happened. Sometime in the night an egg would break, a wet chick nudge its head through the shell. Hens are born with thousands of tiny germ cells, each one a potential egg. And each of my aunts was born with 400,000 ova. When the girls got older, they probably all bled at the same time each month. That's what happens, scientists say, when women live together. Five daughters swimming under the same moon. Imagine. No wonder Grandpa Clarence often slept under the stars after a day of haying.

Two days ago, I visited my father and took a walk with him. "My warranty's run out," he said, laughing but not really laughing. His heart operation years ago was more serious than my aunt's, and the plastic valve was guaranteed only for five years. Walking with him, I tried hard not to think about this, so hard that I *did* forget for a minute. I walked too fast, and as he hurried to keep up, his valve began to audibly click. Love and fear rose in my throat, decades of words I should have spoken.

Ruth is seventy-seven years old but still beautiful and somewhat vain. She wears a scarf at her neck to hide the wrinkles. Once she was a model, and she is still tall and graceful. "Always wear shoes that match your stockings and skirt," she says. "That is the key." If my father had been a woman, he would have been my aunt. Maybe this is why I have come; she is as close as I can get to knowing him. I see my father's chin in her chin, his nervous hands in the flutter of her hands straightening a pleat or refolding the napkin, his eyes in her eyes when she looks away, unable to stay grounded in the moment. I do the same thing. Even as she speaks—now she's finished with the incubator and is onto the caul—I am jotting it all in my brain. The moment is never enough for me. I am never wholly there. I justify this unattractive trait with the fact that I am a writer. Every experience is material.

The waiter has brought our chicken salad, served on lettuce leaves ruffled like the edges of a doily. My aunt has become very talkative and I take advantage of it. "I don't know how much of this is true," she says like a little boy relishing a naughty joke he's been warned not to repeat, so of course I lean forward. "Your Grandma Goldie had a sister. Aunt Cille. She was born in a veil." My aunt says *veil* but I translate it as *caul* because this is what books call the membrane that wraps the heads of some babies. I should use my aunt's word. It is more beautiful and more mysterious. "So she had powers," my aunt continues. "Plus she was the seventh daughter of a seventh daughter, so she could see things other people couldn't. That's how your grandma first knew she would marry your grandpa. Grandma was about sixteen at the time, and one day she and Cille were sitting together in the outhouse, a two-seater. Suddenly Cille said that a man was on the road and he was the man your grandma would marry."

As it turned out, my future grandfather Clarence *was* the stranger on that road, arriving with a team of horses. It strikes me as ludicrous that this is how my pristine father was engendered, that the romance between my grandparents began in an outhouse, foreseen in the crystal of a young girl's eyes, a great-aunt I would never know. I don't say this to my aunt because I am afraid she will take it wrong. There is something solemn in her expression. Perhaps to her also, this moment is more than this moment. We aren't just an aunt and a niece eating chicken salad in a department store restaurant; something is being written here. *All these bits,* she seems to say. *They matter. Don't let them die.*

This is my justification for prying. Because of course it finally comes around to sex, and the discussion of sex across generations always qualifies as prying. I don't ask for the information directly. It starts as a research question, generic, something an interviewer on a talk show might ask. "I heard you and Grandma were midwives, that you helped other farm women with their babies." This is what my father once told me and it seems a harmless question, but by the time she finishes answering, I will know more than I'd wanted to know.

Because it wasn't quite like that. I should have guessed. How could my father have known what went on in the birthing room? He was a young man, out in the fields with my grandfather and the other sons, but already plotting his escape from the farm. Later he would father nine children, two of whom would die in the womb and one as an infant. Six would live, but he would not be present at our births. It was not his fault. In those days, men simply weren't present. They paced in waiting rooms, walking the edges, the perimeters that marked the women's place. The closest my father ever got to the blood of it was when my mother almost hemorrhaged to death after the birth of my sister Lana. He didn't know I was watching, but I was eleven and curious and afraid he was keeping something from me. So I stood at the bathroom door and watched him kneel beside the tub, sloshing her blood-drenched nightgown in the water that was quickly staining to pink.

This is what I'm remembering as my aunt begins the story. "No," she says. "I only helped with one birth. Jack's." Jack is her brother, two years younger than my father. My aunt was seventeen and still living on the farm, the year before she left for the city and a job. Grandma's labor started earlier than expected, earlier and faster, too fast for the family doctor to get there. I am trying to imagine this—watching your mother give birth, delivering your own brother. There are lines we draw, and this is one I have trouble leaping. I have come close. I was present at the birth of my nephew. I held my sister's hands and looked into her wild eyes and calmed her when she screamed that this was a bad idea, that she wasn't going to finish this, that the baby was tearing her apart, was killing her. But a doctor was there, wheeling around on a low stool, taking charge.

My aunt says she doesn't remember much, just helping Grandma onto the dining room table and hearing the screams and seeing the blood, all that blood. Maybe my aunt's head was so filled with hate there was no room to store the memory. "Hate for Dad," she says, for she had decided at the moment Jack was born that this was all her father's fault, that she hated men and that she would never have children. Never.

"But we knew nothing back then," she says, and suddenly she's telling me that her two children—the parents of those smiling grandchildren whose pictures flank her television set—were accidents that would never have happened if she'd known how to prevent them. I have suspected this all along, for in this, my aunt and I are the same: We like our lives well ordered and under control. You can see this in the careful way we dress, the schedules we keep, our early to bed, early to rise, one-a-day-vitamin mentality. Which is probably why I never had children. Sometimes, mostly in dreams, my body mourns what never was, those 400,000 ova floating unfinished, but most of the time I live in my head, not my body. This is my father in me, not my mother. And it is my aunt. If my aunt had lived my life, she would have been childless. And if I had been my aunt, married early in the days before the

Pill, I would have been the one with two accidents. I would have been the one laid out on that same dining room table where three years before she had watched her mother give birth.

Yes, this is the real story, the one that breaks it all open: Fifty-seven years ago in Illinois there was a blizzard. This is not exactly the way she tells it, but I am doing the math in my head as she speaks. She was barely twenty, married less than a year and living out her pregnancy. Because, short of killing yourself, there is no way out of this contract. The baby *will* come. She was visiting her parents and because of the blizzard, her husband could not get to her. "Or wouldn't," she says, after all these years still not sure. The doctor had been notified, but it was doubtful he would make it in time. When the contractions started, Grandma helped her onto the table. For two nights and three days she was in labor. Outside the dining room, Grandpa walked the floors, stomping and cursing, knowing that if no one else arrived, he would have to help. He had never been this close to the birthing room before and if he hadn't thought his daughter might die, he wouldn't have been this close now.

At the last minute the doctor did arrive, but Grandma couldn't hold my aunt down by herself and Grandpa was forced to help. The doctor finally pulled the baby out of her. It took eleven stitches to sew her up. "I felt every one," she says. Her father was holding her head, his rough farmer hands tight on her temples. When it was over she looked up to him and, "as hateful as ever I said anything," she says, and her teeth clench on the memory, "I said 'You did this to Mother too.'" Later Grandma told her the dining room had looked as if a hog had been butchered there.

When my aunt finishes the story, her eyes are lit with pain and I sense without her saying it that she never forgave her father.

Not to his face. Not while he was alive. Knowing my aunt (because I know myself and I am like her), I assume that she never forgave herself for what she said. And she probably never spoke her love, even when it pushed to the surface, even forty years later when it was *he* who lay helpless, attached to an oxygen tank. I decide at this moment that when lunch is over I will call my father, wake him from his nap if necessary, and say the words.

The waiter brings the change and lays it at my aunt's elbow. We stand to leave, then suddenly she sits down again and, as if she doesn't want our time together to end on a minor key, here comes a last remembrance, too small and ragged to be called a story. "One year at the beginning of the war five of us came home for Christmas." (That would be five of my grandparents' children, accompanied by their spouses and families. By then, both of my aunt's children would have arrived safely on this earth.) "The day before Christmas, Dad butchered a hog." She says this as if it were a miracle, something accomplished at great sacrifice, and indeed, for those lean times, it was. "He gave us each a tub of lard and some pork. A real treat. We lived on it for months." She begins to laugh and cry at the same time and her brother my father and my grandfather her father, the one she loved but never until this moment forgave, both sit down at the table with us. This is when I know that long after my aunt is dead, I will carry her inside me. Like a snowball that starts small at the top of a hill and barrels down, I will collect these memories, and when I am her age and rolling toward death, I will roll faster, heavier with her stories, carrying the weight.

life and death, yes and no, and other mysteries in mansfield, ohio

IT'S THREE A.M., and I'm lying with a Zen handbook on my chest, trying to feel no and yes at the same time, trying to see no not as a negation, but simply as a different form of yes. This kind of thinking makes me dizzy. I like boundaries: left, right; no, yes; awake, asleep. If I were in my own bed in North Carolina, I would be fully asleep, on my left side, dead to the world. I would not be reading *No Barriers*. In fact, I own no such book, but it was the only book on the night table, planted by Doug, my host and friend. Doug is a philosophy professor, and he is to blame for my insomnia. At dinner, he spoke of mysteries. Not the Agatha Christie variety, spun and solved within three hundred pages, but the *essence* of mystery. "What constitutes a mystery?" he asked. "How do we know when something is a true mystery, and when it's simply a paradox or a problem?"

"It's easy," I told him. "Everything on earth—and below and above—qualifies. The entire universe is a mystery: electricity, Jell-o, the soul, permanent waves, sex, death, black holes, computer chips."

Ever patient, Doug shook his head and took another sip of

wine. He's been contemplating the nature of mystery for twenty years, and is in no hurry to solve it. Perhaps the question itself qualifies as a mystery. Another question that occupies Doug's mind is the nature of waiting. What constitutes waiting? Is it active or passive? How do we know when we are waiting? Before his questions, I thought I knew what waiting was. I'd ordered linguini with red sauce, I was starving, and it took twenty minutes for the waiter to bring the food. Waiter: one who waits. Is this an active waiting? When a waiter waits on a table, what exactly is he waiting for? I was fine before Doug started in with his mysteries. Now, six hours later, I am half awake, or half asleep. Is this some kind of punishment? Do philosophers, when their children misbehave, send them to bed without answers?

MORNING comes too soon. The blinds are halfway open, and lances of sunlight pierce the room. It's Sunday, I remember. Seven, if I can believe the clock on the night table. My eyes are gritty, and my mouth feels as if a bird has nested there. It takes me a moment to remember where I am. Yes, there is my suitcase, leaning against the low wall that slopes from the narrow ceiling—an attic room, paneled in a dark wood called wormy chestnut. According to Doug, a disease several decades ago killed all the chestnuts, but it's possible their roots are still alive. One day, the trees may be resurrected.

I stumble to the window and pull the cord on the blinds, blinking against the sight: It's the Holy Mother, tall and sleek and white, her arms outstretched. A blue grotto partially encloses her: Venus on the half shell. Beside her is a freshly dug grave, its black dirt heaped at her feet. I reach for my glasses to erase the vision, but it is no vision. It *is* the Holy Mother. Doug's house, I now see, backs up to a cemetery, less than fifty feet from my window. It's just like Doug to live beside a cemetery. The living and the dead, next-door neighbors. No barriers, except for a tall chain-link fence that loops the perimeter of the lushest grass I've seen in months. Golf courses and cemeteries have the greenest grass, and old cemeteries like this one, the most beautiful trees.

When I was a child, my grandparents' farm adjoined a small country cemetery, and Great-aunt Bessie took me for evening walks inside its iron gates. Cemetery prowling was her hobby, one that began in childhood and continued throughout her long life. She would point out unusual stones, stoop to squint at the inscriptions. If she'd known the deceased, she'd bring forth some remembrance, good or bad—she was not superstitious about speaking ill of the dead. If the deceased was a stranger, she'd make suppositions. "Hm. Nineteen. Beloved wife. Must have been childbirth." Or, "Let's see, 1917. That would make him thirteen. 1917. Influenza, I presume." It was on these walks that I first learned subtraction. In the classroom I'd relied on finger counting or bead sorting, unable to carry numbers around in my head only to erase them one by one. But after a few summer evenings with Aunt Bessie, walking among the graves, I became a subtraction whiz. Alicia McCormick: Born 1944, Died 1952. Fifty-two minus forty-four: eight. She was eight years old. "My age," I called out, amazed. "Or nine," Aunt Bessie would say. "It depends on her birthday. You've got to take into account the month—the day, too, especially if it was a baby." I avoided the infant graves. I didn't like thinking about dead babies. We'd had one in our family, a little girl named Sylvia who died the year I was born. I didn't yet know that Aunt Bessie had given birth to a stillborn child, nor would I have known what to do with the knowledge.

If cemetery prowling is hereditary, I inherited the gene. A cemetery is my favorite place to walk, ride bicycles, sketch, and write. When I travel, I always scout out the nearest one. In Pittsburgh, I found it three blocks from the hotel, enclosed in the courtyard of a Presbyterian church. The graves were raised concrete slabs that had cracked and split from exposure to time and the elements. In Silver City, Nevada, it was Boot Hill, a lonely windswept boneyard; in Bermuda, a neatly mown lawn dotted with pristine, white-washed stones; in England, a garden overgrown with roses and foxglove, the graves seemingly an afterthought. My penchant for cemeteries has followed me coast to coast. I've walked the symmetrical rows of Arlington National Cemetery and the unnaturally green acres of Forest Lawn, situated too close to Hollywood for me to believe the dead are actually dead. Inside granite mausoleums, movie stars are stacked in drawers. I imagine their bodies perfectly preserved, wax museum alter egos neatly coiffed and rouged, waiting for loved ones to make their weekly visits. It's a passive waiting, I imagine, one free of worldly anticipation.

THE QUESTION of whether there is life after death is so elementary, and unsolvable, as to qualify as a true mystery. Even small children debate the question. After my nephews' dog was buried, they argued about her whereabouts. The eight-year-old was adamant that Funny Face had gone to heaven; the nine-year-old, that she was in the ground and would stay there, period. My sister explained to her sons that they were both right. Although Funny Face's body had died, her soul would live forever. Jennifer's answer was standard parent fare, the same doctrine our mother had handed down decades before: Our bodies will wear out and die, but our souls will ascend to heaven, a place filled with rejoicing and light, one big happy family reunion. When I asked my mother how we would recognize each other without our bodies, she said not to worry, it was all in God's plan, we would know each other by our souls. Her answer was little comfort. Just the week before, as I'd walked home from the barber shop after my summer shearing, my best friend ran past without speaking. If Babs, my best friend, didn't know me after only a *haircut,* how would she recognize my heavenly body, that mysterious being my mother called a soul?

Now, walking alone in early morning toward the gates of Mansfield Cemetery, it occurs to me how long it's been since I've worried these childhood questions. Ironically, the longer I've remained on this earth and the closer I've moved toward the grave, the less concerned I've become with whether there is life after death. The more interesting question seems to be whether there is life after *life.* How to remain vital, to the end? How to live comfortably in the body without relinquishing the soul? Some mornings, just the thought of pulling myself out of bed, brushing, flossing, showering, shampooing, then lugging this body around all day, exhausts me. Other days it's as if part of me is floating on the ceiling, looking down on the body performing its daily tasks, circular and repetitive. Primitive peoples believed that the soul momentarily detaches from the body during sleep; if so, perhaps sleep is for the soul as much as for the body. Maybe the soul is just taking a short vacation, a much needed rest.

Down the length of this street, old mill houses, flayed of white paint, sink into dirt yards, or yards given over to chickweed and crabgrass, except for an occasional bald spot signifying the territory of dog. Or the space where a child's wading pool, like this one, half filled with muddy water, recently sat. Only remnants of life remain. The whole neighborhood appears to have been evacuated, the soul lifted right out of it. Is everyone sleeping? Where is the posse of dogs whose yelps penetrated my dreams? The emptiness makes me shiver, despite the sultry July heat. The only sound is the whir of a rotary fan from an upstairs window. At my feet, a torn garbage bag spills its contents: coffee grounds, soggy newspapers, soup cans, broken toys, soiled plastic-coated diapers.

Doug, an ex-hippie who serves as my social conscience, would probably attribute my uneasiness to class distinctions. "Would you feel this way in an upper-class suburb?" he'd say. "With manicured lawns and enclosed garages and central air-conditioning?" Appearances mean little to Doug. His needs are few, his wants fewer. Even his body, slim and elongated, seems to suggest his minimalist leanings. His house is modest, as is his salary, which goes for books and backpacking excursions, simple yet nutritious groceries for his family, dog treats for Annie. He is not, to paraphrase the Gospels, laying up treasures on earth. In the area of material values, I am not as evolved as Doug; appearances matter to me. I sweep my front walk, paint the window trim when it begins to chip, cut my hair every six weeks, weed my closet of out-of-date clothing. Perhaps I sacrifice too much to these pursuits, energy and time that could be spent reading or singing or making love, but I don't seem to be able to help it. To me, maintenance of the here-and-now is essential, one of many duties required of the living.

I continue toward the cemetery, stepping over an empty pizza box. A Domino's franchise, which was a mill house in an earlier life, squats on the corner. When I reach the end of the block, I'm within view of the cemetery's gate. In the middle of a dirt yard, a

Pontiac Fiero is propped on wooden blocks. Across its rear wind-shield a large sticker screams, in red and black, NO FEAR! Probably the name of some rock group or clothing manufacturer, but the warning strikes me as misplaced. Fear is not something I carry into cemeteries; only the living can harm me. As if reading my thoughts, a Doberman, chained to a pole beside the last house, rouses from the dead, jerks against the chain, lifts his square black head, and snarls, making me think of the dog in the old science fiction movie who guarded the entrance to the underworld. According to Doug, the Babylonians didn't need a guard dog. Their "Land of No Return" was protected by seven walls. If you wished to enter, you had to penetrate all seven gates, abandoning at each gate a part of your earthly apparel, a kind of cosmic strip poker. Once the last gate had closed, you were free of worldly attachments. Perfectly naked, perfectly clothed for eternity.

NOT FAR within the gates of the cemetery, two roads diverge: white Catholics to the right, white Protestants to the left. Recent graves for blacks are rare, scattered among the Protestants', although an older section, near the highway, contains hundreds of blacks' graves, most dating from the early part of the century. Segregation of the dead is an American tradition, suggesting that even in death, we don't wish to mingle. Like calls unto like; each man knows his place. And if we can do nothing to prevent the commingling of souls—Gilgamesh reminds us that in the house of dust, all souls are jumbled together—at least we can ensure that our bones will rest in a fitting neighborhood. In Mansfield Cemetery, the web of subdivisions is intricate. Within the Catholic half, there are sections reserved for Irish Catholics, Italian Catholics, German Catholics, Polish Catholics, each with its particular ethnic flavor, the Italian graves being the most showy.

Within the Protestant half, graves are grouped not so much by ethnicity as by surname. Family plots—though their existence may represent a selfish act of exclusivity, the ultimate *us versus them*—have always comforted me. The sight of a family plot erases, if only momentarily, the reality that death is solitary. Father, mother, and children sleep, as they did in life, close together—even, in the case of family crypts, under the same roof. Ancestors snore nearby. And even those excluded, by fate or biology, from the earthly nuclear family often find a suitable partner in death. Not far from the entrance gate is a two-headed stone, its shared inscription economical and universal: on the left side, *Nephew;* on the right, *Uncle.* No one, it appears, wants to be buried alone.

And few would choose to be left alone, to be forgotten by the living. It's barely eight o'clock, yet already the survivors have arrived—bringing store-bought wreaths, pinching back blooms on flowering shrubs, weeding around the graves, puttering. Two men and a woman are standing beside a truck, which is parked on an incline near the German Catholic graves. As I get closer, I see that one man is thin, sixtyish, with hair so wispy it lifts with the slightest gust of wind. The woman is squat, "of peasant stock" my grandfather used to say of people built solidly, low to the ground. Her head is covered with bright yellow curlers beneath a torn hair net, and I imagine, from the pinched look on her face, that she has slept on these curlers, a Saturday-night ritual, and that she'll rush home just in time for a comb-out before ten o'clock mass. In cemeteries, I invent lives for the living as well as the dead.

The second man, whom I take to be the couple's son, retrieves a shovel from the truck's bed. He's built like his mother, and his stance, in thick hiking boots, is no-nonsense. By now I've reached the incline, and I nod in greeting, waiting to take my cue from them. Some cemetery people prefer to be left alone. New mourners, those who stand quietly near raw graves where grass has not yet been established, often build a wall of silence, but most cemetery people look my way when they see me coming. Some smile or wave, perhaps assuming that I am a fellow survivor. Sometimes they ask me directly about my loss, and on occasion I've been tempted to lie—to invent a death that would invoke their sympathy or camaraderie.

"Good morning," the thin man says, wiping his forehead with a handkerchief he's pulled from a pocket. "It's going to be a hot one."

"Too hot for digging," the son says, looking petulantly at his mother. She must have talked him into this.

Since they've made the first gesture, I venture forward. "Are you planting something?" A benign question, I think—and stupid. What else would they be doing?

"Nope," the thin man answers. The son is leaning on a shovel beside a large lilac tree that shades two simple granite stones. "See that tree? We're digging it up. My mom wants half in her yard. She says she wants to enjoy it while she can. That's her stone beside his." My grandmother used to tell me not to wait until she was dead to send flowers. Send them now, she said. I didn't listen.

"It's a beautiful tree," I say. "I hope your mother enjoys it."

I continue on the pathway, and when it splits, I take the shaded lane leading into the center of the cemetery. Huge oak trees form an arch, spreading thick branches high above my head. Some must be nearly two hundred years old. Looking straight up, I can't see their tops, only a lattice of sky. It's hard to imagine how deep their roots must be, how intricate the underground webbing. The world beneath our feet is powerful and mysterious. I've seen headstones that, over time, have shifted place, and concrete burial slabs split in two from the force of tree roots. But it would take an underground behemoth to move this gravestone—a massive block of marble, at least six feet wide, shaped like a heart. An eternal valentine to a family named BOYKIN. Four names are carved, side by side, into the marble: Michael Joshua, Emilia Kate, Ernest Thomas, Sarah Marie. Quickly I calculate the ages as Aunt Bessie taught me, concentrating solely on the elapsed time between the dates rather than the dates themselves. Michael was three; Emilia, four; Ernest, six; Sarah, seven. My God, I think. How could a family bear this? Soon, other thoughts are tumbling. How did they know to divide the stone into four parts? When the first child died, did they simply give in to fate, tell the mason to go ahead with one big stone, saving space for the rest of the children? Then I notice the year the inscriptions share: 1979, the expiration date for each child. They must have died together—a car accident, house fire, plane crash? But who was watching them, where were the parents? There are no adult Boykins buried nearby, so the parents must have survived. A fate worse than death, I think, to be forced to live past such loss. When her infant daughter died, my mother stopped wanting to live. But within months life swept her up, its current too strong to resist, and within a year I was born. Some women are that way. Wedded to life, they refuse to take no for an answer.

Tanya Matthews must be that kind of woman. I assume she's still alive out there. At my feet, her sons' headstones are side by side, and no math is required to calculate their ages, since minutes and hours are never recorded on headstones. Yet I can't help but count the months between their deaths: nine. And I can't help but imagine Tanya—I see her as a young, sinewy, fearless woman—plunging back into love and motherhood. One of my friends, eternally upbeat, keeps a magnet on her refrigerator: *Say yes to your universe.* I tell her it's unrealistic, that there are times when nothing but no will do. You're going against nature, I say. In response, she loans me self-help tapes to listen to when I drive. *No matter what happens,* the cheery voice chants, *say yes! If you lose your job, if your mother dies, if your husband walks out on you, say yes. If the universe gives you cancer, as it did me, say yes to the cancer. Embrace it. Turn the no into a yes.*

FOR LUNCH, Doug's daughter stir-fries vegetables in a wok. She's home for the summer, working at a department store to help pay her college expenses. Doug's wife is in Maryland. A week before I arrived, her uncle died unexpectedly (do we ever expect death?) and she has gone to help sort through his possessions and prepare the house to be put on the market. She calls every evening—worn out, Doug says. "There's so much stuff," she tells him. "It just keeps multiplying. He saved everything, even boxes and paper towel rolls. Hundreds of ties. And letters. I don't know what to throw out." She'd hoped to finish the sorting in a few days. Now, she says, it looks more like weeks.

While his daughter dresses for work, I help Doug with the dishes, telling him about my morning walk, how I discovered, near the headstones of Tanya Matthews's sons, dozens of infant graves clustered together. I've seen the phenomenon many times, but it never fails to move me. It's as if the infants have more in common with each other than with the grown-up dead. Doug nods. In some cultures, he tells me, there are no funeral rites for babies. He explains that the early Greeks performed no libations for dead infants, believing that the child had little share in bodily concerns, having recently been translated from pure soul, and hastily returned to that state.

He walks to the living room and pulls a thick book from one of many bookshelves. "Plutarch," he says, as I settle onto the sofa. "Read his consolation to his wife. I've got to walk Annie." Annie is a black Labrador, and although her full-grown body is muscled and strong, her soul is a puppy's. Doug rattles the dog chain and she's here, skidding in on the linoleum, dancing in circles around his feet. Everything is new, everything's an adventure, eat the world, yum-yum, and look at that morsel on the couch! One leap and she's on me, licking and slurping, her wet paws in my lap. I've always wanted to be a dog person, since dog people seem more open and loving than cat people. But it's difficult to go against one's nature. My brother claims that no one in our family, except for my mother, is a natural dog person. He says we only marry into dog families, the way some people marry into money. My theory is that every person contains a certain predetermined essence of either catness or dogness; a rare few contain essences of both. Catness is caution, privacy, order, mind; dogness is impulsiveness, sociability, chaos, body. And more body. Animals sense the essence of a person's catness or dogness and set about to balance the scales. Cats, upon sniffing a person lacking catness (usually those who are allergic), will immediately pounce on him, rubbing their white fur against his black sweater, or their black fur against his white sweater, as if to say, "I am the other part of you. Your catness has not yet been defined." In my case, it's the dogs who come—bounding, slurping, panting, drooling.

When Doug leaves with Annie, I brush the black hairs from my shirt and lean back onto the sofa cushions, smelling of dog. I open the book to the first century and begin to read. Apparently Plutarch's two-year-old daughter has just died, and he's away from home, writing this letter to console his wife. It sounds more like an admonition. He's telling her not to show too much emotion, but to be modest and sensible in her grief. Remember the joy the child brought us, he says, rather than the sorrow. Easy for him to say, I think. He's been on the road, he probably never even held the child. "It is an impious thing," he continues, "to mourn for those who are so quickly translated to a better region. . . . The soul which remains in the body but a short span and is then liberated quickly recovers its natural form."

Do we still believe this? Is this why we engrave children's headstones with "Little ones to Him belong" or "Sleeping safe in the Shepherd's arms"? As if infants and young children are more closely linked to heaven than to earth, to soul than to body, as if their deaths are less the crossing of a difficult barrier than a natural absorption through a semipermeable membrane. An infant's obituary, if it exists at all, is poignantly brief. "Not much to list, I guess," Aunt Bessie used to say as she studied the morning newspaper. The child has been in the world too short a time to acquire titles or possessions, or even, in most cases, any mark to distinguish her as an individual, apart from the inimitable fingerprint or footprint. Near the end of the letter, Plutarch seems to be struggling to remember something, anything—a characteristic, a memory—that would set his daughter apart from other children. Finally he lights on one, calling forth the times when the daughter would "invite her nurse to offer her breast not only to other infants but even to furnishings and toys in which she took delight," as if she wished to share with them "the good things she had."

EVEN IN DEATH, perhaps especially in death, we long for distinction, and though I understand why a military cemetery like Ar-

lington, with its rows of identical white crosses, encourages conformity over individuality, I've always detested such conformity
in civilian graveyards. The Indiana cemetery where my grandparents are buried is modern and efficient as a factory, its rows of
look-alike stones laid flat against the ground, evenly spaced to allow for carefree maintenance. Even the inscriptions are regulated
into sameness by a board of directors, and the only officially
sanctioned grave ornament is a sturdy metal vase, anchored to
the ground, which can be collapsed for easy storage on mowing
days, when bouquets must be removed. No trees obscure the order of the scene or cast uneven shadows over the graves. No
leaves litter the neatly edged walkways. If the purpose of a cemetery is to maintain perfect order, to put its inhabitants in their
respective places and sweep the scene of any hint of life, then this
cemetery has achieved deathly perfection.

In contrast, Mansfield Cemetery is disorderly, chaotic, and
flamboyantly alive. Except for the lines between Catholic and
Protestant, between black and white—lines that have become
blurred with the most recent graves—there seems to be little dis-
cernible pattern to the layout. Certainly there are no straight
rows. Graves cluster beneath wide-leafed oaks, curve around
culs-de-sac. New graves are jigsawed into place, squeezed between older graves, each one seemingly unplanned, as if death
came as a surprise to all concerned. Yet however haphazard the
scene, there are no signs of neglect. Even the most modest graves
are well tended—no easy task given the uneven terrain, the
humps of hills and hundreds of shade trees extending as far and
wide as I can see. If a crew of contract workers maintains the
grounds, the crew must have been trained by an old-fashioned
caretaker, like the elderly man I met in England who lived in a

cottage at the edge of a rural cemetery. More than usual care has been taken here, in part, I see, by the families that cruise the winding lanes, the back seats of their sedans blooming with over-size wreaths and bouquets. It's late Sunday afternoon, and I imagine that the families have been to church, eaten their fried chicken dinners, and changed into cemetery clothes. I'm back, trying to walk off a large serving of Plutarch, and thinking about—what else?—life and death and the barriers between. Is death the welcome destination, and life merely its waiting room? Is death the gateway into the real self, into the individuality we are deprived of in life, burdened as we are with worldly expectations, the sheer physical exhaustion of keeping up? Or is death the final erasure of personality? Who are we, finally, apart from our names, our possessions, our clothing and hairstyles? Stripped naked at the seventh gate, will we be recognized?

The Sunday afternoon families seem to have settled these questions, opting for death as distinction; no look-alike graves for them. Car trunks open to reveal spades, shovels, flats of marigolds, American flags, college banners, yard ornaments, and mass-produced shrines. A plump middle-aged woman is kneeling at the base of a birch tree, pulling up leggy pansies, a six-pack of impatiens at her feet. She looks up as I come near, but she does not speak. Beside her is a simple pedestal marker made of a strange pinkish stone, around which she has constructed what amounts to a miniature suburban yard. A wooden bird, anchored by two stakes and a rope, holds out stiff wings that will transform into whirligigs with the first brisk wind. A concrete Dutch boy is kissing a concrete Dutch girl. And a tiny Virgin Mary, painted fluorescent blue, watches over the scene.

All over the cemetery, still lifes, similar to this one, abound. It's as if the families have reconstructed a portion of the loved one's life, something to accompany him on his journey, to remind him of what he left behind. Or perhaps the individualized shrines are for the living, a way of connecting with the deceased, sharing a piece of his heaven. If heaven exists, these still lifes seem to say, perhaps it is not so different from earth, after all. Maybe, like the ancient Japanese heaven, its landscape is the same as ours, and located nearby, easily accessible by way of an ordinary bridge. If heaven exists, I'm thinking, I hope it's maintenance free. Look at this man, his back bent over a headstone, scrubbing furiously with a wire brush he's dipped into a plastic bucket. He's dressed for labor, in a worn jogging suit and soiled sneakers. A buzz haircut, speckled with gray, asserts itself above a bandana he's tied tightly enough to leave marks in his forehead. He looks up as I approach. "Morning," he says breathlessly, between scrubs. He's leaning, like an athlete, into each stroke.

"Looks like you've got your work cut out for you," I say. Cemetery talk is mostly cliché; anything else risks intimacy. I usually try to maintain a proper distance, but I'm curious about this act: *scrubbing* a headstone? People often wipe the stones with towels, or dust them with handkerchiefs. Some hose down the stones with garden hoses belonging to the maintenance crews. Once I even saw a woman cleaning individual letters with Q-tips. But scrubbing?

"I take care of ten graves," he huffs. "Six of my wife's family's." Gasp. "Four of my family's." Pause for breath. "This one here's my wife. She's been gone nine years." He leans forward, rubs the brush across her name, then sits back on his heels. "This stuff's not working," he says, gesturing toward a plastic container of Joy detergent. "Hey, you wouldn't know how to clean gravestones, would you?"

"Sorry," I say, then remember the patio bricks I cleaned last spring. Muriatic acid? Uriatic? I hesitate, flip through my brain for connections. I'd hate to get it wrong—one cleans bricks, the other defiles them. Once I dated a boy who hated his dead father so much he swore he pissed on his grave every chance he got. Urologist, uric. "Muriatic acid might work," I say. "But you should ask the groundskeeper first."

"Thanks," he says, standing to dump the sudsy water onto the ground. "I'll do that. You have a good day now; I'd better get back to work."

I look back at the man. He's rubbing his neck as if in pain, and the knees of his sweat pants are muddied and misshapen, permanently distended from his long habit of kneeling. Nine years is a long time, I think. He could have remarried, maybe even had children. He could be on a picnic with a new wife, or playing catch with a son, instead of here, scrubbing headstones. After the loss of her baby, Aunt Bessie never tried again. She took no as the universe's final, and personal, verdict. Late in life, she recalled the sensation of holding her breath, trying not to take in too much air, air that should have been her child's. Bessie lived for nearly one hundred years, never totally relinquishing the feeling that she was taking up too much space in the world, breathing too deeply air she didn't deserve. A hundred years is a long time to hold one's breath, a long journey toward the next world.

Near the end, she began to shrink. Every year when I'd see her at the reunion, she'd be a little smaller. My uncles used to say that if she kept it up, they'd be able to carry her in their hands. Bessie loved the attention, loved being the center of a story, even if it meant she had to recycle the same tale over and over, as she often did, ending with a laugh and her signature coda, "I'll never forget that if I live to be a hundred." She couldn't resist a joke. One morning, looking up from the obituaries, she gasped dramatically and turned to me. "They've finally discovered the leading cause of death."

"What's that?" I said, playing my assigned role of straight man.

Bessie put the paper down and leaned forward as if she were about to reveal the mystery of the universe. "Life," she whispered, and threw back her head and laughed.

Above my head, there's a scramble in the branches. A squirrel leaps to a lower limb, carrying in its mouth a shock of dried Indian corn, the kind you see in Thanksgiving centerpieces. Probably an arrangement someone forgot to remove. The squirrel, Robin Hood of the cemetery kingdom, is taking advantage of the opportunity, robbing the dead to feed the living—in this case, the squirrel babies I hear, rustling above in a nest. Trunk lids are slamming, cars are starting up. I glance at my watch. Nearly five o'clock. I want to be back in time to help Doug with dinner. His daughter gets off work at six, and she'll be hungry. As I walk the lane leading to the gate, a pink Cadillac passes, so close I could reach out and touch it. The driver slows so as not to swirl dust in my direction, and I wave in appreciation. A woman's arm appears through the window, encircled by a chain-link of silver bracelets. The arm is shapely and tan, the fingernails freshly polished in bright red, and as she lifts her arm in a slow-motion wave—the kind you see in parades or coronations—the bracelets jangle all the way to the gate.

the weather

ELEVEN YEARS since the Christmas blizzard, and still my sister wakes, remembering. "How could we have been so stupid?" Claudia says. "What were we thinking, to let the children out in such weather?" I tell her it's too late to worry now. Besides, it could have been worse. "You weren't there," she says. "You can't know what we went through." Then she's telling it again, her mantra, her chant, counting the details like rosary beads, as if, by mere repetition, the memory can be exorcised.

It was December 1989, and my three sisters and their children—seven of them, at the time—had gathered at my parents' Indiana home for the holidays. There was the usual mix of excitement and dread, the intermingled joys and terrors of an extended family's extended holiday. The weather was treacherously cold, with wind chill factors below zero, and the children, held hostage by the weather, were even more manic than usual—fondling and sniffing the wrapped gifts, arguing over whose pile was the largest, who kicked who first, who got more Coke in their glass. The women made jokes about the fated Donner party, each placing her own spin on the tale, one sister suggesting the headline "Housebound Clan Resorts to Cannibalism, Three Children Missing."

When it snowed the second day in a row, the children, native Californians and Carolinians, were ecstatic with the possibilities. For Lana's daughter, three-year-old Hanah, it was the first snow, and she reacted with the appropriate childhood clichés. She pressed her face to the window, looked out, pointed, clapped her hands—pale delicate hands laced with blue veins—and begged her mother and aunts to please let her go out and play. The other children egged Hanah on; they'd been whining all day, to no effect. Their mean mothers, their mean aunts, wouldn't let them out. "It's not that cold!" the children cried. "We'll bundle up, we promise." The children kept on all afternoon, until in desperation one of the women—no one wants to claim this distinction—caved in to the demands. Okay, she said. But just for a minute. The children were duly bundled and mittened, their faces covered with scarves and ski masks, not an inch of flesh exposed. They'll be back in two seconds, my sisters agreed. As soon as they feel that wind, they'll come running in. "Stay in our yard," the women cautioned. And the children were out the door.

It is Claudia telling the story, not Lana, who is Hanah's mother, because Claudia was the first mother out the door, running bootless, hatless, to answer the screams. When she got to the field across the street, her own daughter was running toward her, carrying Hanah. In one instant, Claudia looked down at Hanah's bare hands, scooped Hanah into her arms, and began running toward the house. It all happened so quickly yet simultaneously so slowly as to qualify as one of those moments that forever redefines one's life. Animal instinct took over as Claudia tucked Hanah's right hand against her breast and put the other hand into

her mouth, all the while running, praying silently, promising anything—her own life, her own hands—in exchange for the safety
of this screaming child.

My mother and other sisters were waiting at the door. Lana
took her daughter from Claudia's arms and rushed her to the
sink to plunge the stiff blue hands into water. Hanah's high-
pitched cries pierced the air, then someone was on the phone to
emergency, calling out procedures to someone else, and the rest
of the children appeared at the door, stomping snow from their
boots, demanding to know what had happened, why was everyone crying, where's Aunt Lana taking Hanah? My father, who'd
been unaware that the children had been outside, was suddenly
furious with fear, rushing to the driver's seat of the Chrysler.
"What were you thinking?" he shouted to Lana as they backed
out of the driveway and headed toward the hospital.

IN JULY 1995, the Midwest was sweltering in temperatures of
well above one hundred degrees, and once again the family had
gathered at my parents' home. Holed up in the air-conditioned
house—all six siblings this time, along with spouses and fourteen
of the fifteen grandchildren—we shook our heads and clucked at
our bad luck. A year ago, when we'd begun planning for our parents' golden wedding anniversary, we'd debated the wisdom of
hosting the event on the actual anniversary date, January 28. Indiana winters are notorious, and our family had known its share
of canceled flights, impassable roads, frozen pipes—and frostbite.
Over the decades, some incidents had become legend. Fifty years
before, our parents' wedding had been marred by biting wind
and cold; a few years later, when their infant daughter was buried, the road to the cemetery had been snowbanked and rutted,

making car travel impossible. My mother, too weak and despondent to attend the service, had stood at a window and watched the procession of horse-drawn buggies. The horses' breath, she remembers, was white against the leaden sky.

As it turned out, January 1995 was unseasonably mild, and the morning of my parents' anniversary bloomed sunny and windless. Six months later, we gathered around the hearth of CNN and watched as officials updated the crisis from heat watch to heat warning to heat emergency. The newspaper carried daily precautions: drink fluids; avoid alcohol; don't waste money on fans, they just move the hot air around; slow down; wear cotton; stay inside. "Right," we said. "Seven families in a split-level?" It was the Donner party again, this time in reverse. The heat index rose to 125. Cattle and pigs and horses lay dead in country fields, their bodies swollen and distended. In Chicago, five hundred people— mostly elderly, living alone in cramped, stifling apartments—died over the weekend. (The death toll would later be revised to more than seven hundred.) In Mill Creek, Indiana, the ground became so hot that rails buckled from the heat, throwing train cars from their path.

The Old Farmer's Almanac might have predicted the heat wave of '95 and steered our family from a July celebration date, had we bothered to consult it. Certainly my grandparents would have. But, unlike our ancestors, we don't design each day's tasks to match the color of the dawn sky, the shape of the clouds, or the creaking in our joints. My Great-aunt Bessie, an inveterate journal keeper even at sixteen, began each entry of her 1897 diary with a bow to the weather gods. *Friday, January 1, Rainy. January 2, Rainy and disagreeable. January 3, Cold and blustery.*

And on it continued, each day's litany of weather: *Foggy. Light snow falling. Windy and cold. Warm, thawing. Unusually bright. Nice shower in afternoon.* Sometimes the poetry Bessie memorized in school came to her aid, plumping the daily entries, which, left to bare-boned prose, tended to monotony. Thus, on a quiet evening at home, just back from an exhilarating outing, it was *Jingle, jingle, clear the way / 'Tis the merry, merry sleigh.* And the following morning, the lamps just lit, she looked out onto the new snow and wrote: *How grand is the Winter! / How spotless the Snow, and perfect!*

Bessie's internal weather, as recorded in these entries, usually echoed the conditions of the outdoors. She was an emotional barometer, tuned to the slightest changes in pressure from without or within. Yet even so, she could afford to keep weather at a relatively safe distance. At sixteen, Bessie had another year to snuggle by the fire with her younger sister Sylvie while their parents and brothers braved the elements; another year before she would be forced to quit school and take a job to help the family survive. Bessie would never take up trapping and fishing, as Grandma Sylvie would, following in the tracks of her father and brothers. But within a few years, as the wife of a farmer, Bessie would learn to read the sky—clouds whipping up like a mare's tail foretold a bitter wind, a watery moon meant rain—and to suffer the punishments of the weather. *The blizzard last night was a chilly reception for babies,* she wrote to Sylvie. *We had seven pigs to arrive, have five left by bringing them to the house and thawing them out. Isn't the weather we've been subjected to an outrage anyhow?*

Though hundreds of letters between the sisters, Bessie and Sylvie, are sprinkled with such weather-related outbursts, in the case of their mother's letters, the outbursts become a downpour. In nearly every sentence, Great-grandma Hattie rages against the weather. *These days make one hump around and shiver fast to keep from freezing, have not been farther than the mailbox since Xmas, and here it is Valentine's. My old hens are trying to lay, no luck. Potatoes are as valuable as gold nuggets.* If it wasn't the cold, it was the heat; if it wasn't the drought, it was the floods. Her family's livelihood hung in the balance. *Raining a perfect torrent and the water creeping up on both sides and dark,* one letter begins, the first trickle of a syntactic deluge that continued nonstop: *Yesterday I milked with the water coming in the stable till it was over my feet, we got the cow out and up in the yard, then coaxed the chickens out in the front, pried a board in the wood house, got two more that could not get out, tore a hole in the roof of the cave and Dad went in on the ladder and got out some fruit then we drug things up from the barn and it still kept on coming till it was the highest water that has ever been here, up to the roof of the water closet with a creek running through the garden and the big creek clear up in the yard and still it kept coming up over the bridge.* Here, Hattie takes a breath. *But we are still here, no thanks to the weather. The sun will shine sometime but it is hard right now.*

THE SUN shone again, all right, and the skies sealed up tight. Months later my great-grandmother was on her knees again, this time in prayer for rain, not only for her family but for her neighbors as well. *Anderson's well is dry, Hollidays have to haul water for their stock, even the trees in the woods are dying. There are so many fires one is most afraid to sleep. The elevator burned at Clarks Hill and several barns and Bakers over by Dayton had a field of wheat burnt up and the machine was there, ready to thrash. Jess Smiths house burnt week before last. The bed was afire when they awoke. They escaped with their lives but nothing else.*

In nearly every letter, Hattie was shaking her fist at the sky.

But no weather more enraged her than the ice storm of January 1912. It should be enough that the powers-that-be flood your garden, set the barn afire, wilt the corn crop. Such indignities are nothing compared to missing your youngest daughter's wedding. Just when you've finally accepted the worst—that some young hardware store clerk has spirited away your heart, your baby, your sweet Sylvie, and you've risen at 4:00 A.M. to iron your dress and braid your hair, allowing plenty of time for the twenty mile buggy ride to the church—just then, the weather gods begin their torment. And since you're powerless—you're no Demeter, you can't halt the seasons, plug up the heavens, your daughter is lost and that's that—all that's left to do is write a letter bemoaning the events of the wedding morning, a letter that takes two days to reach Sylvie, who is now a married woman: *Daddy had shaved and primped up and I baked you a cake and chicken but brother came in froze stiff, he had started to Mulberry went to cross the creek up someplace on the bridge, there was ice all over. It was so bad Daddy could hardly get to the barn so we just set around all day like we were at a funeral, felt like it too. The dog howled all day.*

If the elements were conspiring against my grandparents' joy on their wedding day, Sylvie and Arthur didn't seem to notice. Sylvie awoke in a cozy room in her sister's home in Gladden's Corner, Indiana, where the wedding would take place. Arthur caught a Big Four train to Stockwell (it takes more than a blizzard to halt the Big Four), then rented a two-horse carriage to take him into Gladden's Corner. In my grandfather's memoirs, he didn't mention the absence of his in-laws. Instead, he recorded the beauty of the snow from the train window and the blaze of the wedding fire in the hearth, its reflection flickering in my grandmother's eyes. *It was a sign of happy things to come,* he wrote.

A bright beautiful afternoon, but not nearly as beautiful as Sylvie. The gods smiled on us that day.

THE WEEK before I married the boy my father tried his best to love, the rains began in Southern California and would not stop. You have to know Santa Ana, the city where our family lived in the sixties, to fully appreciate this portent. Santa Ana shares its name with the hot dry wind that whips through the canyon. A Santa Ana whistles through your parched bones, striking up conversation with whatever it rubs against. Your lips chap, your hair stands on end, your eyes burn from the dust and bits of airborne debris that transform to miniature tumbleweeds, rolling across city streets and catching in the hem of your air-lifted skirt. The wind is a match, setting off fires that begin high in the canyon and make their way down into the foothills, chasing wild animals into suburban yards like ours. The morning after a Santa Ana, it was not unusual to look up from my cereal bowl and see a coyote—fur singed, eyes wide and glazed—standing on my father's perfect dichondra lawn where a sprinkler system maintained a year-round green.

When the rains began, my father turned off the sprinklers. Three days later, as he looked out over the sodden lawn, he shook his head and said he hadn't seen anything like this since Vietnam. He was trying to tell me something I refused to hear. For months I'd felt a strange foreboding, but I set the feeling aside, attributing it to prenuptial jitters. Don't all brides feel sad? Don't all brides fear they're doing the wrong thing? The last few days before the wedding were straight out of a Shakespearean play. Okay, I thought. I give up. Whatever god I've insulted, I'm sorry.

The rains kept on. Puddles grew. Storm drains, clotted with

debris, backed up, filling driveways with water. Our neighbor's shrubs, planted shallowly the month before, sailed past our kitchen window one morning. I began to dream of rain. The church sanctuary was underwater, the minister had gills. He moved his fish lips, setting off a flurry of bubbles, but I couldn't make out what he was saying. My husband-to-be was nowhere to be seen, and I was drowning, weighted down in a beaded wedding dress, gulping water into my lungs.

But I'm no Calpurnia, I told myself, and these dreams are not prophecies. The wedding is not a sixteenth-century play opening in thunder and lightning and fog. Then why this infernal damp-ness seeping into my bones? For days I'd huddled by a portable heater, holding my slippered feet over the glowing coils, thinking *I'll never be warm again.* Had I stopped right then, listened more closely to the rain's thrumming or my heartbeat's thunder, I might have salvaged the next three years of my life and avoided the sting of a cross-country divorce. Instead, packages kept arriv-ing, soaked through to white wrappings, and when the dining room flooded with gifts, my mother set up a card table in the entrance hall to catch the runoff: electric mixers, silver-plated pepper shakers, yellow bath towels embossed with a monogram I wasn't prepared for.

When the morning arrived, as I'd known it would, I zipped the gown and veil and white peau-de-soie pumps into a plastic bag large enough to hold a body. My father slipped galoshes over his wing tips and carried the bag to the family station wagon idling in the driveway. I slipped my stockinged feet into rubber fishing boots, then opened the front door to a gutter-splashing torrent. The windshield wipers were slapping, the parking lights were on, and I remember standing on the front porch, thinking *This is it, this is my last morning.* My father was waiting beside the car, water rushing off his raincoat and hat, his hand on the door latch—so I ran, sloshing through puddles to the car door opening for me.

HANAH, who recently turned fourteen, has all her fingers, though the pinky finger on her right hand is crooked and stunted. The surgeon says it will never look like the others, then reminds us yet again that things could have been worse. My mother nods, remembering. For days after Hanah returned from the hospital, there was a uncanny stillness in the Christmas house. Everyone was focused on her hands. Red and swollen twice their normal size, they resembled knotted stumps or the claws of some fairy tale monster. Soon huge blisters appeared, bubbling the surface of the skin. Hanah sat quietly in her mother's lap, or on the couch near the other children, drowsy from the codeine that had done little to lessen the pain. Cousins, worn from week-long bickerings, curled together beneath afghans, their eyes rimmed with red. Even the youngest spoke in whispers. It was a quality of silence the house had never known, one which the adults, many years later, remember as prayerlike, infused with an eerie calm. Like the quiet after battle, my mother recalls. The children would remember it as interminable—moments, hours, whole days that would later be recovered from one of my nieces' journals: *We waited and waited. It took a long time. We were all afraid.* Over the next week, until they left to go home, the children did not ask to go outside. Boots, toboggans, ice skates were stacked away in the garage, while outside the snow kept falling, falling, white drifts piling high against the window, all that dangerous beauty.

with my father in space-time

I FIRST saw the symbol on the Ben Casey show. Later I sat in al-
gebra class, my pencil skating over the figure eight the teacher
had named Infinity. I traced it, retraced it, and as the line looped
back on itself, I tried to take it in: Infinity. It was not the same as
Eternity, a concept I had only recently begun to visualize. I saw
Eternity as a line stretched out full like a jump rope or a hair ribbon, or marked off in evenly spaced intervals like the time lines
we drew in history class. Eternity stretched a long, long way, farther than I could see on either end—for despite what our minister said, I was certain there were limits in both directions. After
all, God *was* the Alpha and the Omega, the beginning and the
end. Heaven was laid out in golden streets, not circles.

But Infinity? Here was something I had not bargained for, two
circles growing into one another, a snake devouring its own tail
(or the tail devouring the snake). If time *was* indeed infinite, anything was possible. The lie I would tell at dinner that night could
already have been discovered, and the wart the doctor had removed the week before might just now be sprouting below my
skin. If time was not only eternal, but infinite and circular as well,
then it was possible that I had always existed; that I would never

die; that I might be older than my grandmother; and that my own father, who was flying a mission in Vietnam, had yet to be born.

Now, thirty years later in the time line of my life, I find myself in another classroom, at a midwestern university where I have come for a six-week stay as writer-in-residence. I have left behind my husband, cat, job, and kitchen for a converted dorm room with only my clothes, books, and alarm clock for company. On days when I am not conducting readings or lectures, I go back in time and pretend to be a student. I sit in on classes—art history, music appreciation—but it is the Space-Time class that most fascinates me, probably because I have no earthly or heavenly idea of what is going on. It's an honors course, team-taught by a local philosophy professor and a visiting physicist from Siberia whose accent is so thick that his textbook-perfect English must occasionally be translated. Even when the American professor is speaking in familiar midwestern tones, I feel my eyes glazing over. Awash in a sea of confusion, I still—when the professor looks my way, for approval, I am sure, since he mistakenly considers me a peer—nod in numbed assent. I've been here before. *Déjà vu.* This moment detaches from its Now and loops back to another place-time: a Formica kitchen table where my high school physics book lies open, beside the test marked with red ink and labeled "F." My father, on stateside duty this year, spreads his beautifully symmetrical hands across the book as if to caress it, but I can tell by the way his jaw is working that he is losing patience. With a freshly sharpened pencil he carves yet another diagram into a clean sheet of paper. "Now do you see?" he says again. I am biting my lip to keep from screaming. I want to be anywhere but here.

THE PROFESSOR gestures to the physicist, who begins again in his Siberian accent, delivering what he must consider a simplified synopsis of the history of Space-Time theory. Directly above his head, a huge round school clock is mounted on the wall. I take copious notes and at the end of the five minute speech, I am elated, certain that now I finally have it. Here it is, my version of the evolution of Space-Time. At first (with Aristotle and even before) there were three players onstage: Space, Time, and Matter. Then it was concluded that Matter did not really exist. (I've written in my notes: *Where is the matter? What is the matter? That is the question.*) According to John Wheeler and others, Matter is only a distortion of Space, like a little bump. So only two players remain onstage: Space and Time. Then along comes Einstein, who concludes that there is no such thing as either Space or Time, independent of the other. There is only Space-Time—and *it* is most likely curved. If that's the case, I muse, perhaps the shortest distance between two points is not a straight line at all?

Now the philosophy professor is speaking. "Bertrand Russell had this to say about Space-Time. Think about it for our next class." I jot down *Russell* and, always the obedient student, scribble the quotation: "If two bodies are widely separated, neither can influence the other except after a certain lapse of time."

I WAS nearly three when my father returned from Korea, and I demanded to know who that man was in my mother's bed. I would sneak from my trundle late at night and burrow between them. In sleep I would thrash and toss, always in my father's direction, my gyrations culminating in a donkey kick that sent him teetering on the edge of the bed and, once, landed him on the floor. My father insisted my actions were intentional, that I was awake the whole time. I don't remember, but my mother insists it is true, that I kept my father at arm's length for many years. As I grew older, I refused to acknowledge his presence when he was home. Yet each time he left on another overseas mission, I would sulk for days, then write long letters that took weeks to reach him.

ABOVE the physicist's head, the minute hand jumps. Time seems to exist, at least in this instant, for the students are gathering their notes and zipping up their backpacks, which of course do not exist except as clumps of Space-Time. No matter. I follow the little clumps out the door and head toward the library, where I plan to spend the afternoon with Aristotle, Einstein, and Russell. I'm onto something now—*if* Now can be said to exist, that is. If it's not just a place holder, an arbitrary boundary between the past and future.

THE FIRST TIME I felt my heartbeat I was eight years old. My father had been in Japan for fifteen months, and Mother was driving us to the airfield to pick him up. She was wearing the gold brocade jacket my father had sent a few months before. She was also wearing stockings. Earlier that morning I'd sat beside her on the bed and watched her unroll one rose-colored stocking, then the other, pulling them up her white thighs and fastening them to the flaps that dangled from the girdle.

Tom and Jennifer were in the front seat. Their heads sat on

their shoulders at the exact same height, the same angle. The car was eerily quiet. I sat in the back seat between Claudia and Rick, trying to count the trees blurring past, when suddenly I felt it. Eight years in my chest, thumping ninety times a minute, nearly six thousand times an hour, and I had never felt it before. I thought I was dying. I grabbed on to the seat back and gasped into Mother's ear, "My heart's beating! My heart's beating!" She nodded calmly and smiled into the rearview mirror.

BERTRAND RUSSELL, *The ABC of Relativity:* "If two bodies are moving relatively to each other—and this is really always the case—the distance between them will be continually changing."

THE SECOND WEEK of the residency, I begin spending afternoons in the physicist's office. I ask questions, he scratches his head and draws diagrams that make little sense to me. Sometimes a red light blinks on his computer. "Ah, it is my son," he says, and retrieves the message. His computer is connected directly to his son's computer in Siberia. They talk back and forth through the telepathic touch of fingers. Because of the time difference, his son is constantly sending him messages from tomorrow. This makes the physicist sad. "My son is fourteen and growing every day," he says. "I am getting homesick." He taps back his message; when his son receives it in a few minutes, he will be in touch with yesterday.

WHILE OUR FAMILY was stationed in Virginia, an Army plane blew up on a nearby landing strip. In it were five fathers returning from an overseas flight. At school later that day, my teacher called us to a circle at the front of the room. (I attended a public school, but most of the children in my school were from military families.) She removed her pastel glasses and rubbed them on the sleeve of her flowered blouse, looking vaguely in our direction, focusing on the air above our heads. "You never know," she said. "Your fathers are military men. America comes first." Maybe she was trying to comfort us, but I couldn't see the connection. The dead fathers hadn't had time to make a choice between America or their lives. Their plane had simply exploded.

After that day, I looked at my father in a new way. When he was home, I made an effort to memorize little things—his long, tapered fingers, more like the fingers of a pianist than a pilot; the crinkly tracks around his eyes; the graceful way he held his knife when he was cutting steak. Every time he left, every flight, was a rehearsal for the final one. I began to prepare myself. I didn't want to be caught off guard.

So it was always a miracle when he came back. Usually it was in the middle of the night. The other children would be in their beds, but I would have escaped to the living room to join my mother on the couch. We'd lie at opposite ends, the soles of our feet touching, an afghan stretched between us. The light on the stove would be on, and we'd take turns dozing, never quite sleeping, listening for my father's car in the driveway. Then I'd hear the back door opening and the stiff shoes squeaking across the floor, and Mother would be off the couch and in the kitchen doorway, her hair mussed from the afghan, her arms open for him. I'd let them have each other for a minute, then I'd be there too with my hands stretched high around my father's neck, smelling the Sen-Sen on his breath and the leather flight jacket. In winter, his cheeks would be cold. Mother would move to the stove to warm something for each of us—a cup of cider, a bowl of soup. Then I'd sit between them and sip. She would ask questions and he would nod, and in a few minutes the miracle would wear off. Since my father was home again, and alive, I'd make my way to bed and crawl into the cold sheets.

THE THIRD WEEK of the residency, I stop attending the art and music classes. Space-Time is consuming me. I wake in the night with questions that I carry first to class, then down the hall to the physicist's office. He smiles at my questions: Does Time, like a river, move through us? Or do we move through Time? Does Now exist, or is it just the tiny engine that drives us from Past to Future? If Now exists, what shape is it and how do we measure it? How long does a Now last? How wide does it stretch? Is it like one of those huge sweatshirts, One Size Fits All? (The Siberian shrugs at this notion. Now *I've* confused *him,* but I am just getting warmed up.) Videographers count Nows in thirty frames per second, telepathic psychics in transmission time. Mystics can stop time, and Buddhists believe that if you meditate hard enough, you can break time into tiny grains. What is time to a dreamer? To a child? Helen Keller said she knew time was passing because she smelled the apples beginning to rot. My father marks the Nows of his life by the cars he has owned. I've seen the list: There were thirty-two.

I WAS a high school senior and there was a boy named Mike. I believed I would do anything to be with him—even lie. What choice did I have? I was still a virgin, and I had promised myself that I would not be for long. It was a warm May evening. My father had just come in from mowing the lawn. His chest, with its sprinkling of gray hairs, was bare except for the dog tags that he almost never took off.

"It's a weekend retreat," I said, holding out the bogus announcement my best friend had typed on a ditto master and reproduced at her mother's office. My friend's parents would be gone all weekend, and she had offered her house to Mike and me. Sweat dripped off my father's arms and onto the paper. "Everyone in the school chorus is going," I said briskly, avoiding his eyes. "Just sign here." My father took one look at the announcement and shook his head. He didn't go to the phone to check things out, he didn't question me. He just said no. No, I could not go. No, it was out of the question.

I felt the heat rising in my neck. I knew he knew I was lying, and I hated him for knowing. Even more, I hated him for trying to protect me from something I wanted no protection from. I had never talked back to my father, but before I could stop the words, they flew from my mouth. "I hate you, I wish you weren't my father, I wish you were still in Vietnam." The words hung for an instant in the space between our faces. My heart was slapping against my chest. My ears were burning. I lifted my chin in defiance, fully expecting—*wanting*—to be slapped, reprimanded, sent to my room. Something in me needed this marking of the moment, the acknowledgment that I was powerful enough to represent a threat, my rebellion the only weight I could wield against him and his heavy love. I watched the blood rise in his bare chest, rise past his sunburned neck and the jowls that were trembling with rage, past the delicate, aristocratic nose spidered with tiny veins. He stared into me for a long time. His eyes were too blue, the center of a flame, lit with anger and what I now know to be pain. The silence between us stretched, coiled, constricted, stretched again until it filled the room, pushing us farther from each other. Then he turned quietly away.

EARLY YESTERDAY morning, the repairman installed a phone in my dorm room. (I've been getting homesick for my husband, and now I can call him at night.) When the repairman finished and I complimented him on his skill, he answered, "Well, that's one in a row." But how can that be, I thought. Counting is impossible without the second element. Aristotle says that the smallest number is two: "Only a body which is next in a series is akin . . . and bodies which are united do not affect each other. Only those bodies which are in contact can interact on one another."

I COULD never have predicted the quiet way Death would make its initial approach, circling my father's head. He had survived the Atlantic, the Pacific, Korea, Vietnam, had long since hung up his leather flight jacket and surrendered to the domestic leathers of golf bag and La-Z-Boy recliner. Then one afternoon while he was mowing the lawn, the heart attack came. The next day he phoned from the hospital three states away. His voice was the same Saturday-morning-mechanic voice of my teenage years, the one he had used as he leaned over the open hood of my '62 Comet.

"All the pistons aren't firing," he said. "Looks like a bum valve." Then his voice changed. He told me he wasn't sure about the operation. If he didn't have it, his chances of living longer than a few years were one in four. "But valve replacement is serious," he said. "I might not make it."

The next day I left my husband to fly from North Carolina to Indiana, gaining an hour. I wanted to help out, to hold down the fort, as Mother calls it. Answer the phone, make casseroles, mow the lawn that had become my father's new career. My first day home, I botched the job. I had trouble keeping the mower under control, and in my haste I left scars in the lawn, ragged places he would never have allowed. That night I burned the casserole. Finally I gave up, poured more coffee, and sat down at my father's desk, awaiting a call from my mother, who had not left the hospital for two days. The operation had been successful, as far as the surgeons could tell, but my father was not out of danger. I studied the open page of my journal. Sentences trailed off, unraveled before my eyes. Since I'd arrived in the house of my childhood, words had refused to find their proper partners.

Mother came home to rest for a few hours, and I took the midnight watch at the hospital. "It's not over yet," the doctor said. I had never watched my father sleep. He stirred from a morphine dream, mumbled, rustled the covers, and fell back in. The bed was narrow, a child's bed. He must have been a child once. When my memory birthed him, he was already nearly six feet long. Parents have an unfair advantage. I felt cheated out of years and years of his life.

Stories of my father's childhood are few and sparse, lost in the dust storms of the Great Depression, in the creaking plow of his tenant-farmer father and the swaying of Illinois corn. Part the stalks, step through acres of black loam, through years of typhoid and smallpox, to a tiny kitchen and poverty's water-gravy, dip a foot in a Saturday night washtub, and you might see staring back at you a blond boy with a narrow waist and chipped front tooth. Perhaps. Except for a few gray photos, the only physical evidence that my father was ever a child is a crayoned picture his mother saved. He was in first grade. The teacher in the one-room schoolhouse had read the beginning of the Goldilocks story, then stopped at the point where the three bears enter. "Draw the ending," she told the children. "Your own ending."

To the teacher my father's picture might have seemed typical, the generic escape dream of an imaginative six-year-old. Lacking the infinite perspective of the Space-Time continuum, she could not have known it was my father's first flight, his first lift-off and soaring. She could not have known his daughter would one day sit in an intensive care unit envisioning that picture: an open window beside a little bed, white curtains ruffling. The bears are lumbering up the stairs, their furry muzzles dripping with saliva and blood. And Goldilocks? She has leapt through the window and is suspended in midair, her white dress a parachute winging her safely home.

"I DON'T UNDERSTAND," I say for the third time. "It doesn't make sense to me."

The physicist smiles, shakes his head. "It's what in Russia we call *a medicine fact*." Yes, I think. Hard to take. Just accept it, swallow it, it's good for you. The physicist has drawn a diagram of a pair of stick twins and is trying to show me how, if one twin is riding on a moving rocket and one is a ground observer, the ground twin will age faster. I'm not buying it. "I thought you said that all laws of nature operate the same in all systems. How could the rocket twin be younger?"

"*If* the rocket twin could travel fast enough, if he approached the speed of light, he would be younger than the ground twin at the end of the journey."

"Well, no one can move that fast. Why waste time thinking about it?"

The physicist shrugs. This is fast becoming his favorite gesture. "Remember what Russell said about the earth and the stone?"

"No. I don't remember." My head is a stone. Nothing penetrates.

"Here," he says, and points to the notes on his desk. "When two bodies are in uniform relative motion, all the laws of physics . . . are exactly the same for the two bodies. . . . But what if the motion of two bodies is not uniform? Suppose, for instance, that one is the earth while the other is a falling stone. The stone has an accelerated motion: it is continually falling faster and faster."

A FEW WEEKS after I return home from the residency, my parents come for a visit. They sleep in the guest room, two floors below our loft bedroom. Mornings my father emerges in an old robe of Donald's that I'd hung on the bathroom door. Each evening we play cards, talk, and laugh like any two couples. And each night at eleven o'clock Eastern Standard Time, my father and I (the larks of the foursome) begin to yawn. Across the table, we give our partners that familiar look that announces it's time for bed. We all say our good-nights, and in the silent dance of the long-married, weave our separate paths to sleep.

I lie beside Donald on my accustomed half. Soon his breathing changes and his arm, thrown across my chest, gains the weight a body gains in sleep, the heaviness of the dead. One morning we will unwind from each other's bodies for the last time, unaware that one of us is falling faster than the other.

But in a universe of eternal Nows, it is always the last time, always the first. And in this particular Now, this gauzy moment between drowsiness and sleep, my mind lifts off, drifts up and down the stairs that divide my bedroom from the bedroom of my father. Time is a measure of motion and of being moved. Perhaps someone else will be the one to put the last mark on the ones I love. We all hope for a big finish, some image to drill our ending forever into this Now. "The last time I saw my father," we will begin, wanting to call forth some significant moment. "The last time I saw my father . . ." And then, because simple truth compels us forward, "He was wiping off the windshield." Or "He was rinsing out his coffee cup." Nothing much. No matter. Emily Dickinson heard a fly buzz. Finally it is the small things that break us. Once I stood on the observation deck of the Washington Monument. The guide announced that if you were to drop a nickel from this height, it could kill a person standing on the ground. That's how much weight something can gather if it travels far enough.

ARISTOTLE: "Since the 'now' is an end and a beginning of time . . . it follows that time is always at a beginning and at an end. . . . And time will not fail; for it is always at a beginning."

CARPE DIEM is our favorite restaurant (even though, as my husband is fond of saying, "The present's not all it's cracked up to be"). And tonight, the last night of my parents' visit, we are going to dinner to celebrate my father's seventieth birthday. He not only suggests that we take his car, but asks if I would like to drive. I've never driven my father anywhere. I climb into the driver's seat, adjust and readjust the seat, and roll down the window to align the outside mirror, catching sight of my father's face behind me.

After dinner the waiter brings the cake, and I tell my father it's time to make a wish. He pours us each a glass of wine. "I wish," he begins, borrowing not from the future as one might expect of a wish maker, but from the distant past, asking forgiveness for things I cannot recall. "I wish I'd never spanked any of you children." And, "That time I made you pick the briars out of your bicycle tire, I wish I could take it back. It was a cold night; you were tired. I can still see you out there on the carport, picking out each little one." Then finally, "I loved all my children, did you know that? They say I was distant. It was the only way I knew to keep from breaking." I look across the table and tell him it's okay, I don't remember it, it's all in the past, and yes, I always knew he loved me. My father proposes a toast to us all, and Infinity, that perfect figure eight, loops around us, knotting the past and the future into one imperfect Now, even as we lift our glasses.

two autumns, one story

SHE'S ASKING us again, for the third time, if we're sure we want to stay. "Most people don't," she says. "They say their good-byes and then leave." Dr. Grace is businesslike and overly serious, her brow perpetually furrowed. It seems fitting to call her Doctor, though she is nearly twenty years younger than I am. She calls me Mrs., identifying me by my husband's last name rather than my own. If we were anywhere else I would correct her, but at the vet's we are a family: husband, wife, cat. Rabbit, our sixteen-year-old male short-haired mixed breed, is what makes us a family. Without him, we're just a couple. A couple of DINKs, my brother calls us: dual income no kids. Years ago, over dinner, Donald's mother surprised me by saying that if she had it to do over, she would be childless. It was near the end of her life, though we didn't know it at the time—she'd told us the chemo was working. "You were smart not to have kids," she said. "If I'd known in advance . . ." I told her I was glad she *hadn't* known in advance, otherwise she wouldn't have had Donald. "Well, he's all grown up now," she said. "It's water under the bridge."

The office assistant, a teenager with freckles across her nose, enters the room, carrying Rabbit. The gauze bandage on his left front leg is royal purple, bright against the white fur. Though noticeably thin, he holds his head regally. An IV shunt protrudes from the bandage; they've already found the vein, inserted the catheter. This will expedite matters.

The assistant hands him over, and even after all this time, I'm surprised at how light he is. Ounce by ounce, he has fallen away. The fur along his back spikes up from bone. I can count each digit of the primordial spine. Over the past few months, he's devolved into an x-ray of himself, a fossil, long dragon bones down the length of his back. We've tried everything—steak, rainbow trout, cheese, ice cream, all the dainties he used to beg from our dishes. Every morning he limps to the bowl and tilts his head thoughtfully, as if trying to remember why he is there. Some days he licks the food, then looks up at us, his front paws arched delicately in the signature rabbit pose we named him for. In the past few weeks, all he's done is sleep—at the foot of our bed, turned away from us. He no longer purrs when we pet him.

I look across the chrome table at Donald. He doesn't want to do this, but he says if he doesn't see it through, he'll regret it. Tomorrow he leaves for an out-of-state puppetry tour—what if Rabbit dies while he's gone? Donald was on the road when both his uncles died, and his mother. I delivered the news about the uncles over the phone, the way the news was delivered to me. I saved his mother for his return, rehearsing for hours, understanding for the first time the meaning of "breaking the news." Everything is so fragile. One false move and it shatters.

"We'll leave you alone," Dr. Grace says. "Just tell us when you're ready." She closes the door and it's just the three of us. Donald takes Rabbit from me and presses him close to his chest, a fatherly gesture he learned somewhere along the way. Before Rabbit, Donald had never had a pet, not even as a child. His parents wouldn't allow it. "You'll just get attached and then it will die," were his mother's words. The first few years of our marriage, the subject of a pet did not come up. Rabbit simply appeared in the quilted covers of a guest bed where we were sleeping on a weekend visit. Our host, Terry, had planted him there, hoping we'd adopt him. The kitten was one of a litter of six that had been left on Terry's doorstep. "I can't keep them all," Terry said. "If you don't take him, he'll go to the pound."

"I'm not taking any cat. Absolutely not," Donald said. The kitten had crawled into the space between us. He was kneading the covers, nursing on the fringe of the afghan. "What's that on his nose?" Donald said, reaching to wipe off a black spot. From that moment on, until the last day of Rabbit's life, nearly everyone who saw him would try to erase the birthmark that made his face look perpetually smudged. "I can't believe I'm doing this," Donald said. "I should have my head examined."

WHEN the man called with the news about my mother-in-law, he didn't identify himself. He simply asked, "Is Donald there?"

"Donald's out of town," I said. "May I take a message?"

"When will he be back?"

"In a few hours." Donald's father is shy, and in the twenty years I'd known him, he'd never phoned us, so it took a minute for his voice to register with me. "What's wrong?" I said. "Is something wrong?"

"She's dead."

"No," I said, incredulous. Then, "We'll drive down as soon as Donald gets home."

"There's nothing you can do. She'll be cremated tomorrow. There's nothing you can do."

"Of course we'll come," I said. I'm from a large extended

family—*the galaxy,* Donald calls us. When someone dies, every-one comes. It goes on for days.

"No." His voice was stern, almost scolding. "It's best this way. It's what she wanted."

Hours later, when I heard Donald's van at the curb, I hurried to meet him at the iron gate that leads to our townhouse. It was late September, the first dogwood leaves reddening, a chill in the air. I put my arms around him, trying to feel his body through the jacket, and all the careful words I'd rehearsed broke apart. "Your mother's dead," I said.

He did not cry. He poured a Scotch, called his father, talked a few minutes, and hung up the phone. Then he sat down in front of the television. He turned on the remote and clicked the but-tons until Lucy appeared beside Ethel. They were wallpapering a living room. Ethel slathered the wall with paste and Lucy slapped up the paper, covering everything—light switches, phone wires, the phone itself. Laugh track voices were howling. Lucy's phone began to ring, but she couldn't find it, and with each ring she grew more frantic, scrambling along the length of the wires, try-ing to find the phone so she could answer it.

How do you say good-bye to a cat? It's a ridiculous notion, when you stop to examine it. You pet his back, you put your nose to his nose, and then what? Rabbit seems to sense something is wrong, but he's always acted skittish at the vet's, having been poked, prodded, injected, and invaded so many times on this cold table. Whenever we go on vacation and have to board him here, we make jokes about "the slammer," creating scenarios of Rabbit in his cell, *x*-ing out the remaining days with his claw. The chart on the wall shows a double ladder of years: cat and human. Rab-

bit is ninety-five, the highest age on the chart. What do we expect, a medical miracle? When Donald reaches to unbuckle the
collar, the tags jingle in his hands. One tag, issued by the North
Carolina Division of Epidemiology, documents that this cat,
number 163202, has been duly vaccinated. The other, a license
tag with an expiration date of June 30, will outlast Rabbit by
eight months.

Without the collar, Rabbit looks naked. He wriggles in
Donald's arms and, in a sudden burst of strength—where did it
come from?—leaps onto the floor, heading for the window. It's a
tall, narrow window, the only one in the room, and its bottom
pane extends nearly to the floor, accommodating a cat's-eye view
of early October. The sky, seemingly wedged to fit the pane, is
too blue. A small bird pecks in the dirt, inches from Rabbit's
nose. Rabbit's tail tenses, his whiskers twitch. "Maybe it's too
soon," I say to Donald. "He could last a few more weeks, maybe
even a month. Let's take him home."

Donald shakes his head. "There's no sense drawing it out."

Dr. Grace appears at the door, her brow creased even more
than usual. "Sorry for the delay," she says. "No one wants to do
Rabbit." After sixteen years of boarding, he's acquired trustee status among his keepers; the technicians often let him out to roam
the office at night. When new employees, unaware of Rabbit's
status, walk by his cage, he stretches out a paw as if in greeting.
All the technicians now know him by name. "I'd do him myself,"
Dr. Grace says, "but the techs need the practice. Don't worry, it
won't be long. In the meantime, would you fill out this form?"
She hands us a clipboard. "There are four choices. We need to
know your wishes." She closes the door behind her.

Choice #1 is out. We live in a townhouse. Our yard is too

small to serve as a burial ground. Choice #2 is overkill. We won't be making visits to a pet cemetery. Choice #3: A mass cremation? Too anonymous, too heartless. Choice #4: Private cremation; sufficient dignity. We can sprinkle the ashes over the garden.

MY mother-in-law's body was cremated the morning after her death. That had been her wish—the quickest, cleanest solution, she'd decided, one that my father-in-law seemed comfortable with. No announcement appeared in the newspaper. No service was held. My father-in-law asked that we not make the trip. "There's nothing you can do," he kept saying. For the next few days, Donald appeared numb. He did not cry. I phoned close friends and the local constellation of my family's galaxy, who gathered at the townhouse. We displayed photos of Donald's mother, I read a poem, we drank wine. As the glasses were lifted, I asked Donald if he wanted to say something—a story, a memory, anything about his mom. He toasted in silence. A few weeks after the gathering, an urn was delivered to my father-in-law's door. He sprinkled the ashes under the azalea bush in the front yard. I don't know if he said anything, or if he uttered a prayer. Donald and I weren't there.

AFTER A WHILE the bird at the window no longer interests Rabbit. He begins pacing the room, limping slightly on the bandaged leg. According to Donald, cats are the most difficult animals to mimic. Dog puppets are easy—a dust mop will do, just a few shimmies and bumps. A cat's dance is more graceful and mysterious—a stream, a swirl, a ribbon of movement sliding in and out of view.

The door opens and Dr. Grace appears, followed by a gangly

boy-man. "This is Darryl," Dr. Grace says. I've never seen him before; he must be new. He's tall, ponytailed, and extremely nervous. The white coat is too short in the sleeves, and his wrists, dangling awkwardly, are trembling. I pick Rabbit up from the floor and steady the bandaged leg. Darryl's hand goes to Rabbit's nose, trying to wipe off the birthmark.

"No one's looking forward to this," Dr. Grace says, motioning toward Darryl, who is fumbling with a syringe. "Don't worry," she tells us. "This is just clear fluid, to test the line." Darryl squints, takes Rabbit's paw in his hands, and inserts the syringe into the catheter. "Good," she says. "It's clear." She looks at me, then at Donald. "Are you ready?"

Donald makes a strange choking sound, followed by a series of hiccups. He's standing a few feet away, on the other side of Darryl.

"It will be very quick," she says. "It will be like he's going to sleep."

Darryl is holding Rabbit's paw as if they're shaking hands, some stupid cat trick from late-night television. I want to grab Rabbit, run with him out the door. "Are you sure?" she repeats.

I nod. She hands the syringe to Darryl, who looks up at me as if seeking absolution. "It's his first time," Dr. Grace says.

"Tough job," I say. Darryl takes Rabbit from my arms and lays him on the table. His thumb presses on the syringe. Tears are hot in the corners of my eyes.

Dr. Grace leans down, presses her head close to Rabbit's fur. "It's okay," she begins softly, repeating it until it becomes a mantra. "It's okay, it's okay, it's okay." She reaches beneath him and folds his legs gracefully, some exotic dance they seem to know by heart. Even in sleep, a cat dances—the fine muscles rippling, the rise and fall of chest, the twitch of REM. But this is not sleep; sleep, he could manage on his own. It is death we have given him. This is not Rabbit, this puddle of flesh and fur spilled upon the examining table. I pick it up. It's slack, heavier than the cat I used to hold. The hazel eyes stare up at me, unblinking. I close them. Dr. Grace puts the stethoscope to the chest. "We need to make sure," she says. I lay the body back on the table. She listens awhile longer, then takes the stethoscope from her ears. The body releases a deep sigh, another. It twitches. "That's just agonal breathing," she says. "Don't worry, he's gone." By now Donald is weeping, his back against the wall. I cross the room, wrap my arms around him, and begin to rock him back and forth.

the other mother

"WHO WAS SHE?" friends ask, seemingly bewildered by the extent of my grief. Sometimes I answer that she was my mother's close friend. Sometimes I say she was *my* dear friend, but when I explain that we were a generation apart I feel the listener's sympathy deflating, as though a generation's "remove" lessens the power of the loss. What I want to say is, "She was my other mother." This seems the only vessel large enough and deep enough to contain all that she was.

"Now, who was she again? I forget." Had I buried my biological mother, people would not keep forgetting. Theodore Roethke's poem for a dead student, Jane, ends with this outpouring of grief: *I, with no rights in the matter, / Neither father nor lover.* What right do I have to mourn Carolyn's death? If I say I feel I've lost a mother, does this rob Carolyn's daughter of her rightful place on the ladder of mourning? Should I weep in private, wring my hands of her memory? Ours was an unregistered, unofficial relationship, the kind that can't be claimed on income taxes, the kind that engenders what death educators call "disenfranchised grief." (Disenfranchised mourners also include children, whose grief is often not valued; survivors of a friend or family member who died under conditions considered shameful; and anyone who mourns a relationship unsanctioned by society.)

It was not mother love I was seeking in Carolyn. From the first colostrum it was granted me: breast- and hand- and eye-love. Unlike those unfortunate infants who suffer from "failure to thrive," who literally die from lack of touch, I grew fat on mother's milk and attention. Call it happenstance, fate, something the stars tossed my way in the guise of a woman named Juanita, my biological mother.

Jung would have called Juanita my "accidental carrier," a term embedded in the idea that as daughters grow into womanhood, we "must come to recognize 'the human being who is our mother' as the 'accidental carrier' of the archetype." No wonder she gets so tired. Enough to carry *us* for nine months, then another few years, our bodies sleep-heavy, our arms linked simian-style around her neck. But to carry the *idea* of mother, the whole ball of wax? The universe must have known this was too much for one woman to manage. So Mother Earth was born, and Mother Nature, and goddesses and grandmothers and plowed fields and caves and ovens and all manner of scooped-out vessels. At different times in my life, one or another face of the archetype has appeared to me. At one point, my biological mother; at another, my maternal grandmother; then her sister, Great-aunt Bessie. Lately, the face that swims up from dreams is Carolyn's.

MY MOTHER is a down-to-earth, gentle woman, easy to be around and easy to love. She is also emotionally private. Though I am sure she has wept long and hard, I have never witnessed her tears. Her mother was also this way, as were my aunts and most of the significant women in my childhood. Carolyn, on the other

hand, cried easily and often, at times seemingly unable to distinguish between joy or sorrow. Any occasion could bring on
tears—a story, a photograph, a song played on her spinet. "No,
no," she'd say when I'd take my place on the bench, cranking up
Vivaldi, my foot tapping a military beat (Carolyn had no use for
metronomes). "No baroque," she'd say. "Schumann, please. Or
Brahms." But I knew none of the Romantics. My piano teachers
frowned on them, as they did on my tendency to play by ear.
"Well, then, make something up," Carolyn would say.

I'd been punished by teachers for not playing the notes on the
page, and now here she was encouraging me. "Like this," she'd
say, leaning forward, her hands resting lightly on the keys. Music
theory held no interest for Carolyn; she lacked precision and for-
mal technique. Nevertheless, the music came—haltingly at first,
then infused with passion, her tears falling on the keys. If her
husband Walt was home, he'd sit on the couch and listen, his
hand stroking the back of some aging dog or cat.

To say that Carolyn cried easily is not to suggest that her life
was an open book. Like my mother, Carolyn maintained her private places, and in some ways her boundaries were more staked
off than my mother's. You entered at your own peril. The door to
her study, which she called "my inner sanctum," was always
closed, and only a few people "in God's entire world" as she put
it, were allowed in. Inside were rows of books—and when the
rows filled, *stacks* of books on the floor, against the window, on
her desk. Though each room in her house contained items she'd
collected in her travels with Walt, the inner sanctum was the re-
pository of the most precious treasures. Every wall, file cabinet,
closet, and window ledge was filled: beads, shells, feathers, pots,
teacups, bracelets, scarves, handmade paper, hand-painted egg-

shells, weavings. Hundreds of objects, and a story beneath each one. When I picked up a single bead or a shell or a shard of pottery, I was given the tale of its acquisition—the sounds and smells of the outdoor booth, the squint of the seller's dark eyes, the leathery feel of his hands as money was exchanged. And sometimes story layered upon story—the seller's tale, how he'd come to possess the treasure.

During the forty years I knew Carolyn I was allowed into the sanctum only twice. It was not enough to be a loved and trusted member of her inner circle. Your entrance key was also the promise that (1) you would not touch anything unless she gave permission, and (2) you would not pass judgment on the extent of the clutter. Carolyn made no apologies for her style of housekeeping, but she quickly grew defensive if she sensed a visitor's unspoken judgment. My father was such a visitor. A fastidious man, he found it difficult to ignore the stacks of magazines, newspaper clippings on the refrigerator, dog hairs on the sofa. Carolyn's casual attitude toward housekeeping extended to the kitchen table, where cats curled beside your coffee cup and the dog licked the plate you'd momentarily abandoned.

My parents' house—though comfortable and homey, the kind of place where friends and neighbors drop in unannounced, sprawl, and linger—is relatively clutter-free. Like me, my mother is married to a man more enamored of order and cleanliness than she is, and without the influence of our neatnik husbands, both of our homes would probably look more like Carolyn's. Our natural instincts run to collecting, reusing, holding on to objects of emotional value, but unlike Carolyn, we keep our clutter out of sight. Under the watchful eyes of our husbands, every few months we make a clean sweep, reorganize, file away our treasures, which we can retrieve at a moment's notice. For beneath the layers lies an order known only to our minds.

Carolyn was a master of such order. She knew not only the location of each feather and scarf, every letter sent to her, but she could put her hand on it. If something was out of place, she sensed the loss, the way God, in the parable recounted in Matthew, numbers every hair on your head and notes each sparrow's fall. Once while I was visiting during the last year of her life, we sat in the living room, my eyes surveying the small cocktail table. Beneath the glass cover, tiny shards of pottery were arranged on a velvet cloth. They all looked the same to me—nothing special, just broken pieces of clay and glass. Suddenly, in the middle of a sentence, Carolyn gasped, "The Israeli Blue, where is it?" She opened the case and began searching among the folds of velvet, where she found the piece her eye had momentarily passed over. A broken fragment, no blue I have ever seen. Blue, perhaps, only in memory, the color of the sea that washed over her bare feet one morning forty years ago as she waded with her young daughter.

IF THE UNIVERSE accidentally supplied me with a loving and fertile mother (my mother gave birth to seven children), it also twisted this complication: My other mother, Carolyn, was biologically childless, as I am. Thus the world names us. There is no term for women-who-do-not-give-birth that does not emphasize the *without-ness*. Barren, childless, sterile, even the more modern (and supposedly upbeat) *childfree*. In *A Sense of the Morning*, David Hopes writes, "Somewhere I picked up the notion that things must be mine before I can love them." Yes, we pick up that notion early on, never quite relinquishing it. We give lip service to other possibilities (*she was like a mother to me*), but finally, blood is thicker. No matter whom we take into our hearts, how hard we love them, how fierce the extent of our delight and grief, it appears our bonds cannot stack up against uterine ties, the blood that binds.

Nature is a mother. All else is measured against her standard. In my case, Nature and I were like those star-tossed lovers whose paths keep crossing yet never intertwine. The lovers approach one another, dance awhile, fall away, meet and marry others, fall away, meet again, and so the dance continues, the timing always a bit off. When I did come close to motherhood, I *miscarried*. Another unfortunate word, as if women who suffer miscarriages have made some mistake, failed to carry not only the child but the whole idea of mother.

Carolyn carried two children full-term—that is, her daughter and son survive as adults. Both were birthed by other women. She and Walt adopted the children while they were stationed in Germany. (Like my father, Walt was a career military man.) Many years later, Walt found himself once again en route to Germany, this time with their daughter Karen, who was a teenager at the time. "It was Carolyn's idea," Karen told me recently, though that's not the version I remember Carolyn relating; she'd once told me that Karen, in a fit of adolescent rebellion, had demanded to see her "real mother."

"She wanted me to have the chance to meet my blood mother," Karen continued. "She needed to know that my loyalties were chosen, not compelled." So Walt and Karen set off with Eurail passes, visiting Barcelona, Paris, and finally Germany. It was a Monday when they arrived in Frankfurt, and the orphanage where they were to obtain the birth mother's address was closed. "We could have stayed over another day," Karen told me. "But suddenly it didn't seem to matter. I told my father it wasn't that important to me, that I was ready to go back. He was touched, I think. We left for home that day."

I can't know what the birth mother carried all those years, or what the reunion might have meant to her. I'm too focused on Carolyn, on the difficult love her decision required. Carolyn, waiting at home while her daughter embarked on a journey to the other side of the world, half a universe away. The King Solomon story: How would the child be divided, which mother would win?

EARLY ON, I'd toyed with the idea of a different mother, but any full-fledged adolescent rebellion was short-circuited when, shortly before my twelfth birthday, my mother nearly died when my sister was born. Carolyn and Aunt Bessie were both present during the week of the difficult labor and birth, my mother's return home, the midnight dash to the hospital, and three dark days of waiting with no resurrection in sight. Terrified and helpless, certain that my mother was dying, I begged answers from these women. Neither, to my knowledge, had ever lied to me; both were incurably, sometimes brutally honest. "Yes," both said, "she is very ill. No, I can't promise she will live."

Nights, unable to sleep, I walked to the upstairs window and stared down at the street, at the perforated line that divided it. I tried on one possibility, then another. If my mother died, who would replace her? My choices, I remember thinking, were meager. Great-aunt Bessie was too old, too moody and emotionally unpredictable. I could imagine her, as I'd been told she'd often done when she was a newly married woman, suddenly getting fed up, strapping on her shoes in the middle of the night and lighting out for easier pastures. And Carolyn? Would she, like my mother, be waiting for me when I walked through the door?

More important, would she play with me? Sit on the floor, cut the deck or shake the dice, trade Park Place for two railroads? Carolyn had so many interests. What if my science project was due the next day and her study door was closed? Or what if she left in the middle of dinner for one of her classes—a grown woman going to school at night, taking religion and philosophy; what was the world coming to? I'd never seen Carolyn at a sewing machine—did she even own a needle? Carolyn was a good cook; I'd eaten many meals in her house. But was her cooking the kind I could depend on, day after day? Her menus, when she executed them, seemed European, inspired. What about those days when she wasn't inspired? My mother was like the trail cook on *Wagon Train,* capable of daily miracles. No matter what was or wasn't in the cupboard, there would always be a meal.

I also feared that Carolyn might be too hard a taskmaster. My mother granted me plenty of space, as she did all her children. Though she maintained adequate order, she was not strict, and I never felt pressured to pursue a certain track. Opportunities were offered, but not insisted upon. All the children took piano lessons, but after a few years, no one was forced to continue; Rick and I kept on simply because we wanted to. As high school graduation approached and my friends were admitted into prestigious colleges, my mother did not berate me when I made noises about getting a job, maybe taking evening classes at the junior college. She encouraged my writing pursuits but did not push me into English or journalism, and for a few years I changed majors the way I changed clothes, trying on one, dropping it before the mirror, then scrambling for something to suit my present mood: piano, voice, theater, dental hygiene.

Poetry was a garment I tried on early and never totally discarded, though I kept my passion, and most of my early attempts, secret. Outside of English teachers, the first person to whom I showed a poem was Carolyn. I was sixteen, and there were three characters in the poem: the universe, my existential angst/joy, and me. The universe was portrayed first as a huge cosmic womb, then as a potter. I, in turn, was the infant being birthed, then the clay being formed into a vessel. (Looking back, I see the poem was not only sentimental and cloying; it was also technically inaccurate. Unaware of verbs for pottery making, I'd resorted to the woodworker's *carved* to describe what the universe had done to me.)

I recopied the poem in my best handwriting, with my best cartridge pen, onto dimpled blue stationery. When I showed it to Carolyn she gave her full attention, reading it slowly, thoughtfully. She did not tell me it was bad; she did not ask me, as one university professor would a few years later, to "please remove this from my presence, it is fouling the air." She simply pointed to the last line, which read *I am intricately carved*. "I'd make one change," she said. "I'd insert *being* right here, so that it reads *I am being intricately carved*. We are never finished."

During Carolyn's last spring on this earth, she sent a letter saying that the cancer had metastasized to her liver, that she was trying to be hopeful but realistic, that she would like for me to visit. Soon. In the meantime, she was putting her things in order—what did I want? I wrote back that I wanted to have her around for a long time. She dashed back a postcard: "Don't get sentimental on me. Just tell me what you want." In answer, I phoned to say that I'd love to have some of her books, especially the mythology, poetry, and anthropology. "Wonderful!" she said. "Come when you can, we'll go through them together. But when you see me, you can't cry." To be with Carolyn, in the shadow of her death, and not cry? Carolyn, for whom tears were as natural as breathing? I paused. "Okay," she said. "You can cry a little, but not much. We don't have time."

DURING my preadolescence, the place in Carolyn's house that most intrigued me was her bedroom. I'd never known a married woman with a room of her own. My parents always slept together; in my mind, marriage was synonymous with a double bed, and the closed door meant *do not enter.* Once, when our family was visiting friends, my parents were offered twin beds in the guest room. The children of both families made pallets on the living room floor. After the midnight movie was over and I discovered my pajamas were still in the guest room, I knocked softly. When I got no answer, I tiptoed in. There were my parents, curled together in the twin bed by the window, the other bed undisturbed. I stared down at them—my father's face pressed into the back of my mother's neck, his arm flung across her waist. This is what it means, I thought, to be married.

So when I discovered that Carolyn and her husband had not only separate beds but separate rooms, I questioned my mother. "People are different," she said. Having failed to receive a satisfactory answer, I began probing, teasing out scenarios. Maybe they didn't like each other anymore—why else would married people sleep apart? What if they'd *never* slept together, not even when they were first married, and that's why they had to adopt? Maybe they'd had a fight a long time ago and one of them had slammed the door the way I did in my sister's face sometimes and they never got around to making up. Then how to account for the obvious affection between them—the hand-holding, the pats, the occasional loving glances across the room? Did he knock on her door? Did they kiss each other good-night—and what kind of kiss—before parting at the stairs? Was it like having a roommate?

Years passed and the riddle deepened. As I grew into adolescence and beyond, then into my own marriage, their sleeping arrangements came to signify a kind of sanity, a different brand of eroticism, perhaps, the polar opposite of the easy familiarity my parents shared. Does distance keep passion alive? Maybe I'd had it wrong all these years. Maybe there were other ways to love, ways I'd never imagined. The last day I saw Carolyn alive I was kneeling beside the bookshelf in her bedroom while she sat on a three-legged stool, supervising my selections. Her daughter had left for a moment to answer the phone, which rang incessantly those last few months. "Walt is the one I most worry about," Carolyn said. "He loves me so much."

The room suddenly emptied of all sound, as if a drain had been unstoppered, all our words sucked away. I snatched at the first noise I could find, a cliché. "What's not to love?" She turned and faced me squarely, sternly, as if betrayed by my dishonesty, my inability to meet her on her chosen ground. "Plenty," she said. "Plenty."

She was right, of course. Dying people are almost always right—they have no time for insignificant babblings. There is plenty, in all of us, not to love. Yet plenty remains. In the last few weeks Carolyn's edges, always sharp, had become even sharper, honed by pain and knowledge. All was centered on the flame of her impending death. Though not yet finished, she was as close as she would get. I reached with one hand to touch her, my other hand on the books that had filled her shelves and would soon fill mine.

CAROLYN and Aunt Bessie were both avid readers—selfish readers, as I am. My mother, who also loved to read, is only now catching up on the books she denied herself during the years she was raising children. Carolyn not only read every book she could get her hands on, she also took them deeply into her mind—questioning, weighing, reconsidering. Though deeply religious (she taught Sunday School for forty years), Carolyn did not passively walk the party line. She tested every belief, each chapter and verse, her worn King James laid side by side with concordances, the Greek originals, texts by Kierkegaard, William James, Aquinas. And she would argue—at the piano, in the garden, after one of her fine dinners, even before the dishes were cleared and stacked and washed. She'd push aside the platters, stroke the cat's back, and begin the debate with her son, her daughter, my father, or me. Predestination. Proofs for the divinity of Christ. The nature of faith or forgiveness, and why Southern Baptists should ordain women.

At the time, already chafing against the church's restrictions and planning my escape to secular humanism, I failed to see why Carolyn remained loyal to the church. Was it her signature stubbornness? Perhaps it was simply a refusal to relinquish the fight. Though she'd preached from a Baptist pulpit, ordination was denied her; when she applied to be a missionary, she was refused. Her son would later leave the Baptist church, partly for this reason, to become a Methodist minister. He officiated at Carolyn's funeral, held in the Baptist church where she had remained a member, and his words that day were part elegy, part diatribe against the denomination that had tried to force his mother into a subservient role.

I say *tried,* for true to her nature, Carolyn managed to find a way. Though never sanctioned by the Southern Baptist Convention, her missionary work nevertheless thrived. Wherever she and Walt were stationed, she taught reading to children and adults, distributed books, lobbied for the opening of schools and libraries. She also employed maids and other domestic workers (at a more than substantial wage) as a way to help not only her family but theirs. Some of these maids were skilled needleworkers. Thirty years ago Carolyn sent me the most beautiful wedding present I was to receive—a pair of embroidered pillowcases for which, I am certain, the maid was generously compensated.

WHEN I think of Carolyn I think of beautiful things. Extravagant, even. "I love things too much," she'd say. "I am too attached to this world." Her bedroom, at the far end of the main floor, held a twin bed, one half of a matched set. The other half, her husband's bed, was in a small basement room furnished with dormlike simplicity. But while Walt's bed was anchored securely in the corner of the room—a bed for sleeping, plain and simple—hers floated like a small boat in a sea of exquisite clutter. Books, clothes, cards and letters, diaries, collections of hats and beads and jewelry from every continent on the globe. From her bed you could reach out and touch any part of her world, any treasure. And within sailing distance was a closet filled with lace blouses, silk dresses, matching gloves and purses and shoes.

Carolyn did not possess a casual wardrobe. She dressed in stockings and low-heeled pumps, accessorizing with jewelry and

dramatically draped shawls or scarves. This suited her temperament and lifestyle, which I came to think of as "indoor," as opposed to my mother's more active "outdoor" life. Carolyn's
daughter, Karen, refers to her mother's style as "a grand worldli-
ness." My mother's beauty was—and still is—less intentional,
something that happens accidentally on her way to something
else. Though she often dresses up for weddings, parties, and other
occasions, her inborn taste tends to the comfortable; when the
occasion is over, she's hurrying upstairs to change into jeans or
khakis, sweaters or soft plaid shirts. This leaves her free to bend,
to plant, to saddle a horse, lift a grandchild, scramble beneath a
blackberry bush, clean out a shed. "Can you use this?" she'll say,
pushing a crate of dishes or a basket of linens in my direction.
Apart from their sentimental attachment, material things mean
little to my mother. She'll give me anything I ask for.

Carolyn, though equally generous, was more selective about
her possessions. "Now you can't have this one," she'd say, pulling
a silk scarf from an open drawer filled with them. "But any of
these, just take your pick." Even at the end of her life, she remained territorial. On our last afternoon together, we rummaged through bookshelves in her basement library. Each book
was scrutinized individually. She'd hold it in her lap, hesitate,
close her eyes as if recalling the book's place in her life. African
folklore, myth and magic, folk tales from Thailand and India,
feminist theory, the history of the Negro in America, gemology.
"For now, these," she said, gesturing to the left side of the bottom
shelf. Then a grand sweeping gesture that took in the whole
room of books, her fringed shawl draping over the wooden
crates. "When I'm gone, of course, they're all yours."

Through the years, Carolyn gave me many gifts; I never went
home from a visit empty-handed. A string of seedpods from

South Carolina, a turquoise ring, perfume bottles, the cameo pin that had belonged to her mother-in-law. The most frivolous yet intimate gift was a quilted lingerie case with pink tassels. It had belonged to her mother decades before, and it still held a pair of silk stockings in a pale, rosy shade. Though I'd never met Carolyn's mother, I felt as if I had. The portrait over the piano was of a tall, stately woman with deeply expressive, hooded eyes and the full, slightly upturned lips that were Carolyn's. Once, while we were watching a Marlene Dietrich movie, Carolyn began to weep. "She looks like Mother," she said. A grown woman crying for her mother? The sight derailed me. "She was so lovely, I wish you could have known her. How can someone that beautiful suddenly not be here? How can that happen? Just like that—gone."

A FEW YEARS before Carolyn's death, she and I were browsing in the gift shop of a Smithsonian museum where she had been a volunteer docent. I was wearing garnet earrings, and when she saw a garnet necklace under the display glass she insisted on buying it for me despite my protests. "You worry too much about money," she said. "Besides, I get a discount." She hooked the clasp at my neck and stepped back to admire the purchase. "Garnet is the blood stone, you know," she said. "It signifies the deepest ties." Recently, when I looked up *garnet* in her gemology book, I learned that it derives from *pomegranate,* the "apple of many seeds." With its red juice and numerous offspring, the pomegranate is the traditional symbol for the womb and its life-giving blood. The shrine of Our Lady of the Pomegranate shows the Madonna holding the fruit in one hand and the child in the other.

When did Carolyn become a mother? When she first saw her

daughter, her son? Did the pregnancy begin in her mind? Perhaps it occurred in the first tears—of joy or pain—that she wept for her children. The Archbishop of Syracuse once wrote, "A woman who weeps always becomes, in the very act, a mother." A few weeks ago I stood in the shower and cried for my nieces, for all that awaits them. The violence of the weeping surprised me, wave after wave that gripped my belly and brought me to my knees; when my knees no longer held, I sat down hard, letting the water pour over me, a baptism. I'd chosen the shower, thinking that the sound of the water would muffle my tears, which always distress my husband. I imagine him outside the door, pacing, wringing his hands, frustrated at his inability to ease my "hysteria." But this is no medieval terror, no empty womb gone roaming. Emptiness does not contain the power to fill us. Or, as the Archbishop of Syracuse put it, "There has never been a sterile tear." In ancient matriarchal tribes, all females were called mothers, regardless of which woman gave birth to the child. Look around: They're still in our midst. Foster mothers, adoptive mothers, stepmothers, sisters, nannies, teachers, aunts, mentors, grandmothers, godmothers. They complete the archetype, help bear the weight.

THE LAST TIME I saw Carolyn she was wearing a bright red dress and a shawl of Russian design, red roses against a black background. Over the phone she had warned me ("I'm a very sick woman, and I look it"), but even so, I audibly gasped when she met me at the door. Carolyn had always been a tall, substantially built woman who carried herself well. This woman was smaller, thinner. Though her face and neck still retained their dignified, almost haughty lift, her chest and belly had caved in, leaving hollows where there had once been roundness. All afternoon the phone kept ringing—friends, doctors, ministers, neighbors. She was a loved woman, but I suspected that the love had become too much for her. She told me she was craving quiet, solitude, and I took this to mean that my presence was wearing on her. I needed to go, to leave her to herself.

Quickly I finished packing my car—several boxes of books, a sack of Winesap apples Walt had gathered from a nearby orchard, and two framed collages of African tribeswomen that had once hung in Carolyn's inner sanctum. But when it came time to say good-bye, I hesitated, my arm resting on the piano. As if she sensed my reluctance, her tone turned suddenly breezy. "Next time we'll do the rest," she said. "We'll finish that last shelf. How about after Christmas?" Was this some new game, some new place she was leading me? We both knew she would not be here Christmas. Was she trying to protect me? Or was this, finally, the way she had chosen to release me?

I thanked her again for the collages. "They're from the Ivory Coast," she said. "Crafted from torn bits of butterfly wings. Did you notice that?" I nodded. Yes, I'd been studying them carefully for many years—two tribal women in profile, each wearing an extravagant headdress. One woman is framed in gold leaf, the other in crude wood. The younger woman is tall, strong, a child bundled to her back. In her hand is a club-shaped pestle lifted above a mortar, as if about to grind grain for supper cakes. The other woman is smaller, older, hunched. The pestle has become a walking stick that supports her body, the only burden left to carry.

good-bye to all this

"IT'S A LOT like dying," Donald has begun telling our friends.
"Except you get to see where all your stuff goes." He's referring
to the state of our rapidly emptying home. Each week another
room is decluttered, swept free of its past, its stories. I box up
books, dishes, paintings, photos that house our history. Then,
with a black marker in hand, I make my selections, dividing the
goats from the lambs: *NYC Urgent. Goodwill. Garage Sale. Store.
No Rush. Attic, keep dry. Breakable.* The emptying is partly for our
benefit, an attempt to sweep the path clean for the journey
ahead. We'll be leaving in a few months, perhaps sooner if the
sale goes quickly.

The emptying is also for prospective buyers, the strangers who
will soon walk through these rooms. "It's time to start wearing
buyers' glasses," our agent has advised, "to see your house
through their eyes. Your house should look occupied by someone, just not a *particular* someone. Do you understand?"

Yes, I understand perfectly. We want to give the impression
that somebody still lives here—no desperation sale, we're in no
rush, we won't take just any offer. On the other hand, if we continue to fully inhabit this place, we will leave no room for the

buyer's dream. A buyer must be able to imagine himself as the in-
habitant—sitting at the dining room table, filling the bird feeder,
stoking the fire. Our home is a stage to be set, everything polished and gleaming, all the props arranged for the upcoming
show, or *showing,* as the Realtor calls it. "Your house shows well,"
he says as he walks through the rooms carrying a clipboard. "Except for. And maybe. And you might consider. Nothing drastic,
you understand. Just."

"Certainly," we say. "We'll get right on it." Since the money
from the sale of the house must support us for the next year or
two, we can't afford sentimentality. First we remove all that might
offend: incense burners, the photograph of two nude men em-
bracing, the sculpture of bare-breasted crones dancing in a circle,
the Buddhist quotes over my writing desk. Then, item by item,
we hide traces of ourselves, anything that might keep a prospective buyer from inhabiting his own dream: the cat's bowl, my
grandmother's moth-nibbled afghan, Donald's brandy snifter and
pipe.

What is left is tasteful, the way chicken cutlets are tasteful. Or
fish that you buy because it tastes like chicken. A house prepared
for the eyes of others allows only what is tasteful. A home, on the
other hand, is like a family member or a trusted friend, the kind
you don't dress up for. A home has seen you at your worst:
morning breath, worn corduroy robe, feverish head hanging over
the toilet bowl. As you've seen it: cluttered, dust-bunnied, bare-
mattressed, smudged. Why then this sadness, this longing to stay?
A week before the showing, I cry, I scream, I rant, I kick boxes, I
sink down onto the floor of the tasteful, gleaming room and cry.

Donald knows better than to try to console me. "I wish I
could do that," he says, "let it all out, say good-bye. Months from

now it will ambush me, I'm sure of it. I'll be walking in midtown, maybe getting into a taxi or standing in line"—*on line*, I correct him, translating the phrase to its New York equivalent—"and it will hit me," he says. "What have we done, what were we thinking? And it will be too late to go back."

To LEAVE A PLACE you love, you must be willing to go the distance. Once our home is listed, the contract signed, there will be no going back. Our leaving, for the past few months a mere hum on rumor's vine, will be public knowledge. Strangers will call, real estate rubberneckers will slow to stare, voyeurs will walk through our garden and peek into our windows which, the Realtor is advising, should glisten, every room ablaze with light.

"You know you're ready," the agent is telling us, "when you can call it a *house,* not a *home.* Are you sure you're ready?" He doesn't want us backing out at the last moment, after he's taken the photos, printed the brochures, registered the property with Multiple Listing Service, planted the For Sale sign in my azalea garden. *The* garden, I mean. The garden that borders the street. "You're lucky," the Realtor says. "It's a well-traveled street. Lots of eye traffic."

THIS IS not our first house, but it is the first one we've called home. In the other house, where my husband and I lived for thirteen years, our feeling of tenancy went beyond the fact that we didn't own the property. More to the point, we didn't inhabit it. *Inhabit,* rooted in the Germanic *ghabh,* implies both giving and receiving; it is attached to the Old English *forgiefan,* meaning to give up, leave off, forgive. To inhabit a place, you must move in

fully—body and spirit, heart and hand. You must give yourself
to it.

When I first met Donald, he was living alone in that first
house, paying rent to his parents, who owned the property. He
had shared the house with his wife and young son, and though
he and his wife had been separated nearly a year, some of her
clothes still hung in the closet. That was fine with me. I was
barely a year out of a disastrous first marriage, one in which I had
given everything and received, or so it seemed at the time, almost
nothing. To inhabit another marriage was the last thing I wanted.
I was content where I was, subletting an apartment one hundred
miles away in the university town where I was pursuing graduate
studies. One hundred miles seemed just the right amount of distance.

We dated for over a year, spent weekends together at his house,
and cautiously began to consolidate our possessions. (A strange
word, *possessions.* Shades of demonic powers, exorcisms. Do we
own our possessions, or do they possess us?) Then, out of the blue
of a bright November Friday, we drove separate cars to a justice
of the peace halfway between our towns, quickly drew up an
agreement promising as little as possible, and signed a marriage
contract. We did not have a honeymoon, we had a weekend.
Monday morning, very early, I left to drive back to the city
where I would live from Monday through Friday for the next
few years. When my graduate studies were completed, I moved
into Donald's house, and for the next several years we substituted
a safe psychic distance—separate checkbooks, separate lives—for
the physical distance that had once sustained us.

A stranger looking on might not have been surprised that

such a partnership would eventually coax its partners, fearful of *habitation* yet needful of it, farther and farther apart. Now, nearly ten years later, we mark the time line of our marriage at the point of its breaking. "Before the separation," we say. Or, "After we got back together." Our home, the one we are about to leave, marks the place where our separate pasts collided and our life together began. Also the azalea garden, the diamond ring (my first), the cat, and the neighborhood restaurant, Carpe Diem, which we've come to think of as ours.

HOME is a space you inhabit fully, a place where body and spirit dwell. For some people, *home* denotes—even requires—ownership. My father is one of those people. During the course of his career he moved with his wife and children nineteen times, but the only places he called home were the five or six houses he owned. As a child of tenant farmers, he'd been aware that the cramped farmhouses he shared with his parents and siblings did not belong to them, nor did the fields they worked from dawn to dusk.

Which may be why he reacts so personally to the news that Donald and I are selling our home in Charlotte, North Carolina, and moving to, of all places, New York City. Home, to my father, is a place where you put down roots. You do not pull up those roots unless you are forced to. Or unless a larger, more beautiful, place awaits you. An apartment in Manhattan (any apartment, whatever we can find, even if it belongs to someone else, we've decided) is not what my father would consider home.

Now that the listing contract is signed and the stakes of the For Sale sign securely planted, the phone is ringing off the hook, the mailbox is full, and people keep dropping by—friends, family, neighbors, colleagues, each with his own take on the news of our upcoming move. Each person seems to react to the news based on his or her own relationship to leaving, or to change in general, or to heartbreaks that are currently mending, or those that will never mend. A former writing student, a man just shy of middle age, sends a letter with a red stop sign centered on the page and DON'T GO emblazoned in huge block letters. (I learn, a few days later, that he and his wife have separated and that he is now living alone.) My best friend, who has known her share of endings, leaves tears on my answering machine. "Life is change," says my sister Lana, cheerfully offering a dream catcher to hang in my window. "Follow your heart."

My mother's reaction to the news is calm, accepting, exactly the reaction I'd expected. "Moving isn't easy," she says, "but you'll make a home wherever you go." To my mother, home is the people in it and the life lived within its walls: *That was the kitchen I painted Chinese red after Uncle Dale died.* Or, *That was where all the kids had the mumps at the same time. That was the year I made matching Easter dresses for the girls. That was the house where Tommy jumped off the garage roof.* My parents' first home was in Jacksonville, Florida, where she'd joined my father at the base where he was training as a fighter pilot. They lived there two months, in a single room in a boarding house. They weren't supposed to cook in the room, but my mother, intent on serving warm meals to her new husband, used a hot plate, warming canned soup and frying eggs. Since they had no table, they knelt on the floor beside the hot plate to eat their meals. "The food always tasted so good," she recalls. "Those were two wonderful months."

Because, to my mother, home is where the stories are; the nineteen houses are remembered not as addresses but as serial installments in our family's domestic drama. She moves into each new story fully, heart and hand, and when the time is up, she leaves as fully as she once entered. Never regretful—"the past is the past," she says—and never fearful of the next move.

EVERY MOVE I've ever made has begun the same way. I wake in the night, my flesh goose-bumped with sweat, my chest thumping as if a small bird were trapped there. This isn't the way I want to be, aligned with the nay-sayers, the friends and family members who keep calling with advice and warnings. They can't believe, after twenty-five years in this town, that we're going to pack it all in. ("Sell your house?" they say. "Leave your business?" they ask Donald. "But what if?") I'd prefer to side with the cheerleaders, the small band of coaches standing on the sidelines, urging us on. "What courage," they say. "At this time in your lives, to make such a change. Most people move to New York when they're young. How brave of you."

The thumping in my chest continues, a rhythmic *What if, What if, What if.* What if we can't find an apartment we can afford? What if we find the apartment, put money down on it, but can't sell the house? What if we sell the house but can't find an apartment? What if we can't find a home for the cat? What if we can't find work? What if we hate New York?

Donald's night sweats began years ago, but they had nothing to do with moving. And though he didn't voice his feelings of anxiety and sadness, I sensed them. Finally, when I insisted, he spoke them aloud. He couldn't keep on doing what he was doing. He couldn't see himself, ten or fifteen or twenty years down the line, still driving hundreds of miles a week, hauling lighting and sound equipment, setting up stages, pulling the same puppets out of the same trunks, lifting his arms to perform for the hundredth, or thousandth time, the kinds of shows local audiences would pay to see, the shows he would have to perform to keep his company afloat and pay the mortgage on our home. He'd long ago disengaged himself from his work. During shows, he felt as though he were lifting above the stage, above himself, watching his hands perform movements that no longer held any surprise. In the meantime, all the shows he wanted to build—experimental shadow plays, quirky table top shows, toy theatre, object theatre—stayed locked in his head. And he wasn't sure how long they'd hang around.

"Plus," he said. He hesitated, then looked up at me with that half dreamy, half guilty expression in his eyes, the one he always gets when he's visiting the home he carries in his head, his childhood dreamscape. Ever since he was a boy visiting his grandparents in Washington Heights, he has been trying to go back.

"I love our home, you know that," he said, his eyes scanning the lofted ceiling, the crown molding, the oak mantle, and the gold-leaf mirror.

"I know," I said.

"There's just one thing wrong with it."

"I know," I said. "It's not in New York."

Do ALL PEOPLE carry inside them, like a dream wallet snapshot, the image of a place that feels more like home than any place they've ever lived? Why else do we draw dream houses, design blueprints of a space that doesn't yet exist, walk the rooms of model homes, our heads brimming with plans? Let's see, this wall here will be coral, and we'll put a round table in the corner, with a satin tablecloth and stained glass lamp. We can almost see ourselves in the small rocker by the window, a leather-bound book in our hands. No matter that we've never owned a leather-bound book, that our daylight self prefers the casual intimacy of a dog-eared paperback. In our dream house, things will be different. We will be different. Those unused parts of ourselves, the places we've as yet barely touched, will come forth—our pasts, our memories, our future selves. All the lives begun years ago but never nurtured will find their way into this home, even if the home is a studio apartment, a room so small that your bed pulls out from the wall, and your dining table folds down each night to make room for that bed, then opens in the morning to become the desk where you write your as yet unwritten stories, your poems.

In a dream room, everything fits. In mine, there is room for my farmhouse past, for Grandma Sylvie's and Grandma Goldie's wicker baskets filled with "makings," the strips and squares of cloth they will weave into rugs and stitch into quilts. Room, too, for Aunt Bessie's magazines and books and seed catalogs and Grandpa Arthur's hammer and milk bucket and rubber hip boots and Grandpa Clarence's big black Chevrolet and rusting tractor and wire-rimmed glasses and the ashtray that was always within reach, the metal tray weighted with sand and covered in plaid corduroy.

And because I now fully inhabit a marriage, the dream home allows for my husband's past as well. It is a crowded room, half midwestern farmhouse, half Washington Heights one-bedroom flat, Sylvie and Goldie and Clarence and Arthur and Bessie sharing a table with Donald's Uncle Alex, on leave from his travels, and with Donald's Russian grandparents, Boris and Ria.

Donald's young parents are at the table, too, having made their twice-yearly journey with their son and newborn daughter. Like his brother Alex, Donald's father could not wait to get out of New York. When they were old enough to leave home, both brothers signed away their Russian surname and adopted an Americanized version, each setting off on his respective dream— Alex to the merchant marines, and Donald's father to a ranger's station in Oklahoma. "What were they running from?" Donald wonders aloud to this day. "Why did my uncle go to sea and my father to the woods?" Maybe, I'm thinking, home is the place where we begin. The center of the compass, the fulcrum that spins us out.

The dream room is swirling with smoke—my grandfather's Camels, Boris's unfiltered hand-rolled cigarettes. Someone has ordered take-out from the local deli. "Probably my aunt," Donald remembers. "Always the most expensive foods, a real feast, more than anyone could afford but they ordered it anyway," and Boris is getting ready to leave, to pick up the order. But first he must get into his shoes. "It was a big production," Donald says. "Because of the bunions. He had to use a shoe horn, and it took forever."

Later, when young Donald is tucked away on the army cot between Grandma Ria's bed, where his parents will sleep, and the portable crib they've borrowed for his sister, he will lie awake and listen to the grownups laughing, arguing, clinking vodka glasses, talking politics. At this point, I imagine my ancestors, Protestant teetotalers for whom *blacklisted* and *communism* are but dark smudges in their local newspaper, excusing themselves, having picked their way through the unrecognizable smoked meats,

pickled oysters, thick black bread dipped in olive oil from Leba-
non, and bowls of purple borscht dolloped with sour cream.

Lying on the cot with the whole of New York blaring outside
the small window, Donald is smug with plans. Tomorrow he will
put on his best suit and his parents will take him on the subway
downtown for lunch—to the automat, he hopes, where his
mother will retrieve from her pocketbook a handful of coins and
let him choose from the array of sandwiches and fried chicken
platters and slices of fruit pies behind the glass doors. Afterwards
they will go to Gimbel's or Macy's, then to FAO Schwartz.
Donald doesn't yet know that his father will surprise him by
buying a small wooden boat with a battery powered propeller,
and that the day will end more perfectly than any day in his life
has yet ended—at Central Park, on the bank of Conservatory
Lake, where he will wind the propeller as tightly as it will go,
then kneel to place the boat in the water and watch as it makes
its way through the miniature armada of sailboats and battleships
and canoes, each boat followed by a pair of eyes belonging to a
child whose dreams follow the boat across the blue water.

IN Thornton Wilder's *Our Town,* Emily, newly dead, asks the
other dead ones how long it takes before you stop feeling a part
of the other world. A while, they tell her. It takes a while. But
that's not what you should think about, they say. You must focus
on what is ahead. Besides, one of them says, it wasn't so great to
be part of the living anyway. Be grateful it's over.

To leave a home, you must find ways to fall out of love with it.
Those minor irritations that have come to seem, at times, almost
endearing—the rusty gate, the roaring heat pump, the perpetually leaky faucet, the tiles that don't quite match—must be al-

lowed to grow to major proportions. *Thank God we won't have to worry about that anymore,* you bluster to friends and family. *When we get to New York . . .*

And if you must not only leave but also sell the home you love, as we are doing, you must steel yourself against criticisms that might once have cut deeply or roused you to battle. You must dismiss the comments, the offhand remarks from Realtors, buyers, well-meaning neighbors. When you need to fall out of love with your home, there are dozens of people ready to help. Workmen are perhaps the most effective dream busters. *No,* you tell them, *you'd never really noticed that water stain above the chimney. And no, you haven't been up on the roof in years—not since that tree limb cracked during the ice storm. Really,* you say. *That bad?* And the painter, eyeing your faux Tuscan kitchen wall and the plum-colored entry hall, is more than happy to announce how many coats of eggshell white it will take to cover such indiscretions and to provide prospective buyers with a clean canvas.

So by the time King of Steam arrives, you welcome his big cloud-colored truck, the compressor he wedges into your garage between stacks of packing boxes, the thick-as-an-elephant's-trunk hose he unwinds from his truck. You know what's coming. The judgmental eye, the lectures on carpet maintenance and six-month checkups, the Scotchguard recommendations. He's just what you need on this miserable August afternoon in the jungle heat of Charlotte—ninety-two degrees, ninety-five percent humidity, a host of mosquitoes swarming around the bird bath. *Come in,* you say. *What's a little more steam on a day like today?*

But King of Steam has a more intimate relationship with humidity. Although the king is already dripping with sweat, is virtually *glistening,* he refuses the glass of iced tea you offer. He's at least six feet two, and dressed in a checkered shirt and khaki shorts with complicated pockets and snaps, he resembles an overgrown Boy Scout or one of those lederhosened men from cough drop commercials. His calves bulge with thick muscles.

"I see I've got my work cut out for me," he says with a sigh, looking down at the beige plush carpet, which was new when we moved in nine years ago but is not new now. Life happens, what can I say? Now he's warning me that his hose, which he's preparing to wrestle the two flights up to our bedroom, could possibly, just possibly, scratch the wood stairs. "It's my duty to warn you," he says solemnly. When I hesitate, he is quick to point out that it's all my decision, of course, but if this were his house ("And I have a *big* house," he says, "twenty-six hundred square feet, a *nice* house"), he wouldn't hesitate to give permission. "Besides," he says, kneeling on the stairway, "there are more scratches here than these hoses could ever leave. Now, with finely varnished floors, well, it might make a difference."

"Fine," I say. "Be my guest." I sign the release form.

"Scotchguard?" he asks, and when I shake my head, he's off, tripping the light steamatic up the stairs, his hose thumping, step by step, behind him. He flips a switch and the compressor in the garage, two flights down, rumbles into action. In an hour or two he will be gone, taking with him the dirt and grime, the stains, our whole ground-in history—the ink I've dribbled, my nephews' crayon smudges, the Carolina clay tracked in from the garden, stray ashes from Donald's pipe, sloshes of red wine from last month's dinner party, the dander and gray fur from the cat I must soon find a home for.

WHEN you empty a home, you start with what you need least, those items you've either outlived or put away toward some future life you've dreamed of inhabiting but probably never will: the hand-tatted place mats, the satin smoking jacket, doll-size espresso cups, the bamboo vegetable steamer. I once went through a period of believing I would actually wear all the hats I'd bought on rainy afternoons while wandering the aisles of musty antique stores. Hats from the forties, the thirties, the twenties. Hats with feathers and black veils. Then there was my natural-fiber year, when I allowed only silk, cotton, wool, and perpetually wrinkled linen into my closet. If you look deeper into that closet, you will find remnants of the six-month period Donald and I were separated. Skinny from grief and dazed with newfound freedom, I bought short leather skirts, Spandex capri pants, midriff blouses, and slinky dresses with peek-a-boo backs.

Next to go are those things that simply won't fit into the life you are about to inhabit. For us, this means practically everything. Though we've succeeded in finding a New York apartment we can actually afford—a miracle in itself—the apartment is a furnished sublet belonging to friends of friends, a couple who are leaving their possessions behind ("down to the plates and spoons," the wife tells us as she leads us from room to room) to pursue the Hollywood dream they've carried in their heads for years. She opens a closet, its shelves stacked with boxes marked *Xmas, Winter Clothes, Memories, do not crush.* I tell her not to worry, that we'll be careful with her things. "Especially the china," she says, her eyes clouding over. "It means a lot to me."

Our tenancy might last a few months or it might stretch to years, depending on how the gold of their Hollywood dream pans out. This uncertainty as to the length of our stay, coupled with uncertainty about where we will end up—I started to write *permanently,* but how can you ever be sure—compounds the already nerve-splitting stress of the packing process. What to take with us, what to give away, what to store, what to loan? If our New York dream pans out, we won't be returning to Charlotte or to any space large enough to house all our belongings. I like calling them belongings rather than possessions. They are belongings because they belong where they are, in the life we inhabit in this place.

But if I'm ever going to finish packing, I've got to stop calling everything a belonging. *The past is the past:* my mother's voice in my ear. What belongs in a three-level townhouse with a garden and two decks owned by a long-married couple with a steady income is not what belongs in a prewar furnished midtown Manhattan sublet rented month-by-month by a couple of terrified middle-aged freelancers. Something's got to give. Almost everything. The garden tools, wheelbarrow, wrought iron bench, patio umbrella, birdhouses, planters, stereo cabinet, television console, twin love seats, end tables, coffee table, bookcases, bedroom chairs, bureaus, lamps, paintings, mirrors, shelf after shelf of books, the dining room hutch and everything on it, the Stickley table that belonged to my parents, along with the seven Stickley chairs ("Somehow, in one of the moves," my mother recalls, "the eighth one disappeared. How could that have happened?"), the dark cherry bed we recently re-slatted to support the queen size mattress we graduated to on our twenty-second anniversary.

And the piano, my first acquisition as a young bride preparing to leave my parents' home. A piano was the one thing I knew I could not live without. Music was my solace, my companion, the keyboard on which I wrote my first wordless poems. Though I could not remember when my parents had bought their shiny black spinet, the one I'd played throughout childhood and adolescence, I couldn't remember it *not* being there. What is a home without a piano?

So I cashed in my savings account and bought what I could not live without, a used spinet with a Swedish walnut veneer. My father and brothers hoisted it into a U-Haul and unloaded it at the shag-carpeted patio apartment where my new husband and I would spend our first six months ("Are all first years this hard?" I asked my mother) before moving to another patio apartment where we dodged the landlord who kept asking for rent money we didn't have. Despite my husband's protests, the piano went with us to the second apartment, then to his father's house where we lived rent-free for a few months, then to my father's house where I waited out my husband's boot camp months, then to the military base four hundred miles north where he was stationed. After the divorce, the piano went with me to the southern university town where I shared a duplex apartment with a stranger, then to a rent-subsidized apartment I sublet from a single mother, then to a garage apartment, then to the house where Donald had lived with his ex-wife, and finally here, to our home.

The piano is the only possession—the only *belonging*—that has survived all the moves, all the lives I've inhabited since I first left my parents' home. And three mornings after we sign the real estate contract, I wake up knowing the piano has to go. More precisely, I have to go, and the piano cannot go with me. I briefly consider storing the piano in my brother's basement, alongside the other furniture that we hope, one day, to retrieve. But knowing what moisture can do to a piano, I decide against this. My sister Claudia has always wanted a piano, and I consider loaning it to her, then retrieving it when we can afford an apartment of our own, though instinct warns me we'll never be able to afford a New York apartment large enough to house a piano.

Besides, I've never had much luck loaning things out to people. After a while, they start believing that the ottoman, or the fur coat, or the mirror belongs to them, and when I return months later to ransom it, their eyes widen in surprise. "My ottoman?" they say. "But I thought . . ."

Or worse, they take no possession at all, and the object I care for so deeply gets thrown into the back of a closet or toolshed or barn where it rusts or rots or mildews or sprouts weeds or otherwise languishes. Bessie, my grandmother's older, childless sister, once possessed many beautiful things—chests with inlaid wood, solid wood tables and headboards, a hand-carved Victrola, and a mahogany upright with ivory keys. After her husband died, she sold their home to move into a smaller house, then yet a smaller house, and in the process most of her possessions were either sold or stolen; the remaining items were loaned out to friends and family members. On returning from an extended cross-country visit where she had been caring for an aging cousin, Bessie found that the prized piano she had entrusted to a nephew for safe-keeping had been abandoned on his farmhouse porch, exposed not only to the elements but to the caprices of the family cats, dogs, goats, and chickens.

I pick up the phone and dial Claudia's number. It will be a gift, free and clear. No loan, no retrieval. Oh well, I tell myself. The piano would have eventually ended up at her house anyway; it's been written into my will for a long time now.

"Have I got a deal for you," I begin, and within minutes my sister has redesigned her living and dining rooms.

"I can see it now," she says. "It will be the center of our home."

While she's talking, I walk into my living room, stretching the phone cord as far as it will go. The piano is still where it's always been, topped with a dresser scarf that my friend Carolyn, dead now a year, gave me during my last visit to her home. She knew she was dying, knew it would be our last time together. "Take anything you want," she said, gesturing dramatically with one hand as if to include everything—the clothes, the jewelry, the books and the stories in them, her life.

"Oh, I'm so excited," Claudia says. "Remember how it was at Mom's? How we all gathered around it?"

"I remember," I say. "What's a home without a piano?"

Or without a cat. My neighbor two doors down has agreed to take our deck-leaping, mouse-chasing, tree-climbing Mr. Dibbs. It would be cruel, we've decided, to cage him in a New York apartment. Better to leave him to wander his old haunts, to come and go as he pleases. The transition shouldn't be too difficult, we figure, since the floor plan of our neighbor's townhouse is identical to ours. I pack up his bowl, his litter box, his grooming brush, his toys, the igloo-shaped bed he has yet to use—he prefers the pillow where I lay my head—and carry him to my neighbor's door, where she is waiting with cat treats. Dibbs accepts her open arms too easily, and I begin to think maybe this isn't such a good idea after all. We form a pact: In exchange for her generosity, I promise not to allow Dibbs back into our house. "You're right," I say. "He has to get used to his new home. We don't want to confuse him."

The next morning when I open the front door, he is there waiting, curled beside the newspaper. How many of his lives have already passed, pages in a cat's calendar? How many did he pass with us? On habit, I reach to pick him up and take him inside, then, remembering my promise, I carry him down the porch steps and set him down beside the gate.

"Stay," I say.

I hurry up the steps, but Dibbs scurries behind me, close at my heels. I pick him up again, carry him down the steps, out the gate, down the sidewalk to my neighbor's house. My hands want to pet him—fur hunger—but I won't let them. How long will it take until he no longer comes to call? Until he knows we are gone, and lifts his tail and walks toward his other life? I lean down and place him like a package on her welcome mat. "Stay," I say.

THIS EVENING, sitting on the sofa, I study the footprints of the couple who, according to the Realtor, will probably buy our house. They must have come again today, during the hours I disappeared. It's what I do now, my new job. Prospective buyers need time alone with the house, the Realtor tells us. They want to look into closets and cabinets. They want to turn on faucets and flush toilets. Some bring their tape measures. Some bring their contractors. How much will it cost to tear out this wall, refinish these floors, repaint these faux Tuscan walls? Where will we hang Mother's antique mirror?

Each time the Realtor calls, I make a clean sweep of the house—wiping down counters, smoothing the bed, emptying the trash cans, spraying something sweet into the air. Then I walk through the rooms, turning on every light. Finally, I step out of my shoes and vacuum the carpet thoroughly, backing myself out of each room.

Then I disappear. Sometimes I visit a friend. Sometimes I go to the library or to the gym. Mostly I just drive around, slowly circling the neighborhood, viewing my home from a respectful distance, wondering how it looks to those who drive by. When the allotted time is up, I cautiously make my approach to the house. If someone is still there, standing on the porch or walking through the garden, I keep driving. When the Realtor calls with his nightly report, I tell him I don't want to know the details— their names, their occupations, how much money they have in the bank.

Footprints provide enough information for me. It's a kind of rudimentary archaeology. Since King of Steam's visit, the carpet is so clean and fluffy that the imprints are clearly visible, down to the smallest detail. I am able to guess not only the size and personality of the ghost guests (spike heels, sandals, tennis shoes) but also the route of their travels. Did they walk to the kitchen twice, three times? Did they avoid the wet bar?

I sit on the sofa and study the prints of the couple, imagining their lives. The larger prints are short for a man's, but very wide, with a substantial heel print, an expensive logo visible in each heel. He has left several trails, round-trip tracks from the door to the fireplace, the door to the balcony, the door to the window, the door to the phone. Was he measuring for new carpet? Was he phoning his bank? The smaller print—the wife's, I presume— was made by a waffle-heeled no-nonsense shoe. The shoe of a waitress, perhaps, or a schoolteacher. Someone who spends a lot of time on her feet. That's good, I think. The stairs won't be a problem for her. I slip one foot then the other into her prints and stand there a minute. When I step away I can see, centered in her tracks, the fossils of my bare feet.

TO FULLY LEAVE a place you love, you must view it from afar, from across a wide expanse of time, space, or feeling. After a while, the wise ones tell you, you will begin to align yourself not with the old place and those who inhabit it, but to the clean white canvas that awaits your marking. In this way, Joan Didion, having fully aligned herself with California, was able to write, without a hint of remorse or homesickness, of her years in New York City. The title of her essay, "Good-bye to All That," demonstrates the distance she had traveled between then and now, old and new. *Good-bye* denotes an ending, as opposed to *farewell,* the word my best friend insists on using for the party she is hosting for me. *That* suggests a separation; *that* is a place you've already left.

This morning on my customary walk, one of the last I will take in this place, I am thinking about Didion's essay, and as I round the corner by the neighborhood pub, Didion's phrase is in my head. I try saying it to the air but it doesn't feel right. *That* is already far removed—the ice frozen over, the wound healed. *That* is to *this* as *there* is to *here.* I pass the dry cleaner's, the fish market, the stylish brick apartment house where my friend lives, a novelist with whom I've shared tea, lemon-flavored cookies, and hour after hour of talk. He lived in New York when he was young and believes everyone should live there at least once. Then why was he so sad the last time we were together; why was I sad? I wind down the path that leads through the city park near the pink-gabled Victorian house and my neighbor's townhouse where the cat I gave up now lives quite contentedly, it seems, at least he looks content there, sunning himself on her deck with a full bowl of food within paw's reach.

LAST WEEK, the footprints in our carpet grew bodies and names. The contract is signed and the earnest money is in the bank. According to the Realtor, the couple is already making big plans to tear out walls, put in new floors, new tile. The closing is scheduled for tomorrow. I've cried my last tears, I'm sure of it. A few nights ago, while Donald and I sat at the dining room table eating Chinese take-out on paper plates, I began to weep. "I'm going to miss our home," I said. "Aren't you going to miss our home? How can you just sit there, eating?"

He stood up, pushed his chair away from the table, and walked over to me. He reached out with both hands as if inviting me to dance. I stood up and, still crying, leaned against his chest. When I tried to break away, he held me tighter, and when I finally quieted, he stepped back a little, making a circle with his arms, enclosing me, leaving only a small column of air between us. "See this?" he said, meaning the circle in which our bodies floated. "*This* is our home."

Now the floors of the house are empty except for a broom, a dustpan, a few packing boxes, a roll of bubble wrap, and a portable radio whose voices keep me company while I work. The NPR host is interviewing the author of a self-help book that combines ancient Buddhist teachings with tips for coping with modern-day stress. One of the best coping skills, he believes, is humor, so he's telling jokes: What did the Zen Buddhist say to the hot dog vendor? (Make me one with everything.) How can you recognize a Buddhist vacuum cleaner? (It has no attachments.)

I've saved the hall closet for last. It's filled with boxes, folders, bags, old suitcases stuffed with mementos. Most people mispronounce the word. I used to, too, until my high school English teacher corrected me. It's easy to see why we call them *momentos.* We link them with *moment, momentous,* perhaps even *momentum,* the force of motion propelling us forward. The boxes in our closets—filled with love letters, family photographs, old report cards, school records, awards, citations, obituary clippings—mark the moments of our lives, those brief occasions from which our pasts set sail. "A voyage of great moment," one writer called the journey, and it is indeed a momentous journey, weighted with grave implications.

"No," the English teacher said. "It's memento, as in remember. A memento is a relic, a reminder of the past. Related to the Latin *memento mori:* Remember that you will die." When it became clear that Aunt Bessie would soon die, my parents moved her from the log cabin she'd lived in as a child and to which she'd returned after the last of her cross-country journeys, into a spare bedroom in their home. They packed all her remaining possessions into a mahogany chest that stood at the foot of her bed.

After she died, my parents cleared out the room to make space for my mother's parents, Sylvie and Arthur. The accumulated belongings of their sixty-year marriage had been culled to fit into the space of one small bedroom. My parents filled the bureau top with framed photos, and over the double bed they hung the monogrammed gate latch—*Double S Ranch*—that had once marked the entrance to Sylvie and Arthur's hundred-acre farm. Set adrift from their pasts, cut free from the duties and chores that had defined their lives, my grandparents' marriage shrank back to the size of their original union. They had nothing left to do but keep each other company. Which they did quite well, sitting side by side on my parents' sofa like a young couple who are just now beginning to court each other.

IT'S A MISTAKE, the dead ones tell Emily, to go back. Emily doesn't listen, of course. Had she listened to their advice, there would be no play, no rising and falling action, no final act. She is certain that they are wrong, that if she picks a happy moment to return to, a sunny day to relive—she chooses her twelfth birthday—she will not be saddened by what was. As it turns out, her decision only sharpens the sadness. It hurts as much, perhaps more, to return to a place where we were happy. Especially when we look back on that place, as we must, with new eyes. We hadn't meant to change, we'd thought we could hold things as they were. "Don't worry," I tell my brother, my neighbor, my best friend. "We'll be back for visits, lots of them," and I pull out the calendar to show proof.

"Sure," my brother says. "You know you're welcome any time."

"Dibbs will be glad to see you," my neighbor says.

"It won't be the same," says my friend. Darkness, like a sudden cloud cover, sweeps across her eyes, and I sense that already things are changing, have changed, that a door in her is closing, as it must. In six months, a year, two years, I might revisit the scene, but that's all it will be, a visit.

Home is the place where, once you have left, you cannot return. I used to think you could, I mean why not, there's the road to the schoolhouse, there's the fence post where you sat, there's the garage apartment where you typed your dissertation, why not go back?

"It's never the same," my mother said.

I pointed to the small white house with the peeling shutters, the house where I was born. My mother sat behind the steering wheel. At my request, she had driven me out into the Indiana countryside, forty-five years into my past.

"That's not the place it was," she said.

But the photograph was in my hand. It looked the same to me.

My mother shook her head and turned away, and in her eyes I saw the home she had left, the one we'd never get back. It was larger and brighter and sadder and sweeter, swelled up with context: the morning light across the rain barrel, my brother circling the driveway on his tricycle with the metal wheels, the rich compost smells of hay and dust and washing powder and sun-starched sheets, a baby (that would be me) crawling toward the porch steps, and—in the center of it all—a beautiful black-haired woman holding the sheets close to her breast, her eyes fixed on the scene at hand.

acknowledgments

Acknowledgment is due to the publications where these essays previously appeared, some in different versions:

"Aunt" was aired on National Public Radio's *The Sound of Writing* and was later published in *One Word Deep: Lectures and Readings* (Ashland Poetry Press) and reprinted in *The North Carolina Prose Anthology* (Avisson Press). "The Uncles" first appeared in *Shenandoah,* where it received the 1997 Thomas H. Carter Prize for the Essay. "The Riddle Song: A Lullaby in Twelve Parts" first appeared in the *Kenyon Review.* "The Cloud's Immaculate Folds" first appeared in *Crab Orchard Review.* "Dependent" first appeared in *Connecting: Twenty Prominent Authors Write About the Relationships That Shape Our Lives* (Jeremy P. Tarcher/ Putnam), which was published as a special issue of *Creative Nonfiction.* "Earth, Air, Fire, and Father" first appeared in *Alkali Flats.* "Hatching" first appeared in *Life on the Life: Selections on Words and Healing* (Negative Capability Press) and was reprinted in *One Word Deep: Lectures and Readings* (Ashland Poetry Press). "Life and Death, Yes and No, and Other Mysteries in Mansfield, Ohio" first appeared in *Literal Latte.* "The Weather" first appeared in *Quarterly West.* "With My Father in Space-Time" first appeared in the *Gettysburg Review.* "Two Autumns, One Story" first appeared in *Salamander.* "The Other Mother" first appeared in *Crab Orchard Review* and was reprinted in *Sorrow's Company: Writers on Grief and Loss* (Beacon Press). "Good-bye to All This" first appeared in

Fourth Genre: Explorations in Nonfiction, published by the Michigan State University Press.

I also wish to thank The North Carolina Arts Council, The MacDowell Colony, and Ashland University for fellowships and residencies that allowed me time to complete many of these essays.

Thanks also to all the editors who have supported my work throughout the years, especially David Lynn, Dave Smith, R. T. Smith, and Michael Steinberg, and to Sue William Silverman and Malcolm Call, whose enthusiasm for the book helped make its publication possible. I'm especially indebted to Gail Peck for her constant friendship and her straightforward, wise response to early drafts of these essays. Finally, I am grateful beyond words to every member of my family, alive and dead, whose love sustains me, and whose generous acceptance of my work frees me to write the truth as I see it, even when that truth is difficult to hear.